THE GRACE OF GOD

THE GRACE OF GOD

Faith To Receive God's Unlimited Promises

by

Keith A. Butler

Harrison House
Tulsa, Oklahoma

The Grace of God—
Faith To Receive God's Unlimited Promises
ISBN 1-57794-303-1
Copyright © 2000 by Keith Butler
P.O. Box 34546
Detroit, Michigan 48234

Published by Harrison House, Inc.
P.O. Box 35035
Tulsa, Oklahoma 74153

CONTENTS

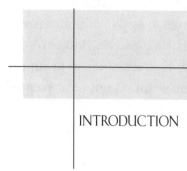

INTRODUCTION

I believe you should not accept the word of a preacher unless he or she can back it up with Scripture. Unless you can confirm something a preacher speaks about in the Word of God, you're under no obligation to receive it. The Bible is our text. It is the Word of Truth. How else are you going to know the truth unless you go through God's Word to find it? You have to spend time looking at God's Word, meditating on it and finding out what it says before you can accept it. That's how you develop your faith.

You see, you can't believe anything unless you're told about it first. That's why you've got to go through the Scriptures on the subject you're going to believe for and see it first. Then you have to meditate on them so they can get down into your spirit. Once they are in your spirit, you have the basis for a belief. That's called *faith*. Faith is simply a belief or a persuasion that something is true.

That's what we're going to endeavor to do in this book. We're going to learn how to obtain the faith needed to receive God's unlimited promises. We're going to march through the Scriptures and take our time studying what it takes to build your faith. We're going to help you form beliefs based on God's Word. We're going to show you how God's grace can help to supply your every need. And once you've found out what your faith can do in partnership with God and His Word, you can expect to walk in the fullness of God's unlimited promises.

CHAPTER 1

WHAT IS GRACE?

Have you ever wanted to see more of your prayers answered and experience more of God's living promises? Of course, we all have. That's what being a child of God is all about. God expects His children to know how to exercise their faith to get results. Because God is a God of faith, He wants His children to be faith "kids." God is pleased when we develop and use our faith to receive His unlimited promises.

God is so eager to see His children blessed that He provided a way for us to succeed even when we occasionally fall short. God has made a fail-safe way for us to enter into His fullness, and it's called *grace*. Grace is the ingredient that allows us to succeed even when we fall short.

Because grace is so instrumental in our walk with God, I just want to look at the word *grace* and go over its various definitions according to the Word of God. It's much easier to discuss a subject when it is clearly defined first, and that's what I want to do with the subject of grace. God's grace is a great blessing, and we need to know how to implement it so that we can benefit from the fullness of God's goodness.

The definition of the word *grace* can sometimes be misunderstood. Many of us seem to have only a nebulous or "murky" understanding of the subject. For example, when something bad happens to someone else, we have a tendency to say, "Well, by the *grace* of God, it didn't happen to me!" Those who use the word grace in this context are technically correct but not fully aware of how grace can affect their lives. There is so much more in God's Word about His grace. We need to know where grace comes from and how we can allow it to operate in our lives. Let's look at some Scriptures to get a better understanding of what God's grace is and where it comes from.

> **Therefore it is of faith, that it might be by grace....**
>
> **Romans 4:16**

> **Therefore being justified by faith, we have peace with God through our Lord Jesus Christ: by whom also we have access by faith into this grace wherein we stand, and rejoice in hope of the glory of God.**
>
> **Romans 5:1,2**

The Bible tells us that it is by faith that we receive grace. Therefore, if it is through faith that we gain access to grace, then we should find out how to use our faith so we can find grace to receive all that God has for us.

God's grace is God's help and favor in times of need. In other words, grace is help from God. Therefore, we can access God's supernatural aid the same way we can access everything else from God—by faith. Our help comes from God and His grace.

Thank God that we have His help! But we can also help ourselves to walk free from sin. We have a part to play in the access of His grace.

> That as sin hath reigned unto death, even so might grace reign through righteousness unto eternal life by Jesus Christ our Lord.
>
> Romans 5:21

> What shall we say then? Shall we continue in sin, that grace may abound? God forbid. How shall we, that are dead to sin, live any longer therein?
>
> Romans 6:1,2

In these Scriptures, Paul tells us that we are *legally* dead to sin. But even though we are legally dead to sin, we must each make the decision not to walk in it. And with God's grace you can do just that. You can decide that you're not going to walk in sin by asking God for the grace to do it.

Many people want others to pray for them so they will be able to resist temptation. Of course, praying for one another is important, but the Bible says we must also resist sin for ourselves. God has given us the grace and help we need in times of temptation so that we can do this. That's grace in the form of God's help.

The decision whether or not to sin is up to you. If you sin, you do so because you choose to for whatever reason. Conversely, if you resist temptation and avoid sin, you do so because you choose not to sin. Do you know why some people can pass the ice cream store and resist stopping in for a double-decker, hot fudge sundae? They *decide* against it. Do you know why other people stop in every day? They don't decide against it. You already have a great deal of power against temptation within yourself. But when you need greater help, the grace of God is there to give you the freedom to resist temptation.

Romans 6:14 says, **For sin shall not have dominion over you: for ye are not under the law, but under grace.** The grace of God is more powerful than sin. The grace of God, God's supernatural aid, is all you need to walk in victory in any area of your life.

First Peter 5:10 refers to God as **the God of all grace.** Grace is not only what God *gives;* it is who He *is!* He's the God of blessing! He's the God of favor! He's the God of help! He is all of these things and more!

THE GRACE OF LIFE

Let's look at some further definitions of grace. In 1 Peter 3:7, the Bible tells us about **the grace of life.**

Likewise, ye husbands, dwell with them according to knowledge, giving honour unto the wife, as unto the weaker vessel, and as being heirs together of the grace of life.

1 Peter 3:7

The Bible teaches that there's a grace of life in marriage. Isn't that wonderful? Married people need God's grace in full operation because it's not always easy to walk in love. There are times that you have to do it by faith. But you have the ability to walk in God's love toward your spouse because of the grace God gives you to be married.

Remember, faith is what gives you access to God's grace. If you have been struggling by trying to make something happen in your own strength, you are not relying on the grace of God. The way for you to receive all that God has for you and to receive it without struggling is to do it by His grace.

GRACE AS BEAUTY

Understanding what grace means will help us to receive everything God has for us, because if we are going to access the grace of God through faith, we need to understand all the definitions of the word *grace.*

Let's look at what the Bible describes as the grace of the beauty of creation.

But the rich, in that he is made low: because
as the flower of the grass he shall pass away. For
the sun is no sooner risen with a burning heat,
but it withereth the grass, and the flower thereof
falleth, and the grace of the fashion [beauty] of it
perisheth: so also shall the rich man fade away in
his ways.

James 1:10,11

Did you know that God's creation is endowed with
grace? This verse is referring to the beauty, or grace, of God's
creation. In this case, the term *grace* is used in connection
with something beautiful. We have all heard the description
of something beautiful as being "graceful." That's what this
kind of grace describes—God's beautiful creation.

GRACE AS THANKFULNESS

At least two translations say that grace is defined as thankfulness and gratitude in the following passage of Scripture:

Let the word of Christ dwell in you richly in all
wisdom; teaching and admonishing one another
in psalms and hymns and spiritual songs, singing
with grace in your hearts to the Lord.

Colossians 3:16

Once you begin to praise and worship the Lord, you will
start to experience a grace in your heart toward Him. The
Bible confirms it. You see, praising and worshiping God

activates faith. And faith in turn activates grace. Therefore, to receive an overflow of grace in your heart, it would benefit you to first praise and thank God with hymns and spiritual songs. God responds to praise and worship.

GRACE AS GOD'S LOVINGKINDNESS

What does the Bible say about grace as God's loving-kindness?

> **And I thank Christ Jesus our Lord, who hath enabled me, for that he counted me faithful, putting me into the ministry; who was before a blasphemer, and a persecutor, and injurious: but I obtained mercy, because I did it ignorantly in unbelief. And the grace of our Lord was exceeding abundant with faith and love which is in Christ Jesus.**
>
> 1 Timothy 1:12-14

In the Twentieth Century translation, grace is referred to as God's lovingkindness.[3] When God forgave Paul for persecuting His church, He was demonstrating His grace of lovingkindness. God gracefully forgave Paul because he repented of his sin.

Did you know that the same grace God made available to forgive Paul for persecuting the church is also ready to forgive you of your sins? God is loving and kind to you all the days of your life. Even when you didn't know Him, He was kind to you. Perhaps you haven't always followed God.

Even then, He was still kind to you. His grace always stands ready to forgive and encourage you. God has always been on your side. The grace of God is His lovingkindness, and we have access to this lovingkindness by faith.

GRACE AS THE CALLING OF GOD

Just as every believer who confesses Jesus Christ receives a measure of faith, every Christian also automatically receives a measure of grace. That's good to know because we need that grace to fulfill our heavenly calling. Let's look at God's grace as the calling of God.

> [There is] **one Lord, one faith, one baptism, one God and Father of all, who is above all, and through all, and in you all. But unto every one of us is given grace according to the measure of the gift of Christ.**
>
> **Ephesians 4:5-7**

Verse 7 says, **unto every one of us is given grace.** In the Twentieth Century translation, this verse says, **Every one of us, however, has been entrusted with some charge.**[4] In other words, every one of us has a calling or a charge. Every one of us has an assignment, and that assignment is the application of God's grace.

That means that every believer enjoys the same opportunity to follow God's plan for his or her life. God allows every one of His children to receive the portion of grace needed to answer his or her call. God wouldn't call you if He wasn't going to equip you with the grace to answer that call.

Isn't God good? As a believer, God's grace already belongs to you. Each of the aspects of grace we have examined is available to you right now. God's grace provides you with His unmerited favor, His anointing, His blessings, His help, the grace of life, the grace of beauty, praise and thankfulness, God's lovingkindness and a heavenly calling. Each one of these types of grace is available to you by *faith*.

CHAPTER 2

ACCESSING GRACE FOR YOUR GOD-GIVEN TASK

God first called me to be a pastor when I was twenty-two years old. I remember that when the Lord spoke to me about being a pastor, I didn't think I could do it. My temperament was such that I didn't have a great deal of patience in my life.

You see, I grew up in the local church—in two different denominations. As a kid, I saw and heard a number of things that turned me off to God. I thought, *If that's what having God in your life is all about, I don't know if I want it.* But I finally gave my heart to the Lord, and God called me into the ministry.

So, when I was twenty-two years old, the Lord said to me, *I want you to pastor, and I want you to open a church.* Then the Lord told me to turn to Romans 10:8, which says, ...**the word of faith, which we preach**.... God told me to call this church "Word of Faith."

I said, "Lord, I can't pastor; I don't have the patience to be a pastor. If these people start messing with me, I'll put my Bible down and hit them in the mouth!" Even at that time I understood what a pastor goes through. I understood that a pastor must have some long-suffering. Pastors have to walk in love with people, even those who aren't always so lovable.

I didn't want to be a pastor. I wanted to be an evangelist or a traveling minister. Evangelists and traveling ministers come into town, spend three days teaching and preaching, love the people and then leave town. I didn't want to stay in the same place and see the same people day in, day out, week in, week out, month in, month out and year in, year out. I didn't believe that I had the ability or the patience to do that.

Not only that, but I was twenty-two. Where I come from, if you're twenty-two, they consider you a boy, and no boy is supposed to be a pastor. So here was my argument with God: I said, "God, first of all, I'm too young to be a pastor, and, secondly, I just don't have what it takes to do this job."

But that didn't stop God from pursuing me to answer His call on my life. He continued to pursue me about it. Eventually, as I continued to read the Word of God, I came to the conclusion that if God had called me to do something, then the ability to do it must be given by God as well. When I started thinking and speaking the way God thinks and talks, I began inching over into faith. In other words, I started to believe I could do what God said I could do. I entered into faith which enabled me to access the grace God had for me to answer my calling!

Do you know what happened? I really didn't have the ability to pastor—not in myself. I just didn't have it. But I said, "Lord, if You want me to pastor, I will do it. I can do it because You said I can." The moment I said these words, I felt as though a cloak had come upon me. It is difficult to explain in words, but all of a sudden, I knew that I had the patience, the long-suffering and the kindness to answer my call. I knew I had the *grace* to be a pastor.

Finally, I took that step of faith and actually became a pastor. The Lord blessed me, and the church grew. I pastored for about ten years before the Lord said to me, *Now I want you to pastor another church; I want you to open a church in Atlanta.* I couldn't quite understand what the Lord was asking me to do. At the time the Lord spoke to me, I was already pastoring a prosperous church in Detroit, with about 10,000 members.

"Lord," I asked, "do You want me to leave the church in Detroit?"

No, He said. *I want you to pastor the church in Detroit and a church in Atlanta* at the same time.

"Lord," I asked, "how am I supposed to pastor two churches 700 miles apart?" But God didn't answer me, and I knew immediately why He didn't. I knew that if He told me to pastor both a church in Detroit and one in Atlanta, then the grace to accomplish that call was already available. I just had to believe God and receive by faith the anointing, or grace, to pastor two churches at the same time. The moment I decided to believe God, I gained access into the grace of God—His calling and anointing on my life. And then I had to act on my faith by doing what God called me to do.

When I began to be obedient to what the Lord had told me to do, I found the grace of God was there to help me do it. I found that I could rely on God's grace to see me through. So, I started pastoring a church in Detroit and a church in Atlanta. On Sunday morning I would preach at the church in Detroit, and later on that same Sunday morning, I would preach at the church in Atlanta. After preaching in Detroit I could take a flight to Atlanta and preach there. I preached at both churches on Sunday mornings. And it worked. Why? *Because of the grace of God!*

I've been pastoring for twenty years by the grace of God. Today I pastor thousands of people in three different churches located in three different states. I pastor churches in Detroit, Atlanta and Phoenix. Some ministers say to me, "I don't see how you can pastor churches in Detroit, Atlanta and Phoenix. Your three churches are over 25,000 miles apart! How do you do it?"

"By grace through faith," I respond.

The same grace of God that enables me to pastor three different churches can also help you do what God has called you to do. Anything God calls you to do, you can do it, accomplishing it by His grace. And you access that grace by faith.

Now, in order to operate in the grace of God, you must first hear from God. In other words, you must either get direction from the written Word of God or from the Holy Spirit. (And anything that the Holy Spirit says to you will line up with the written Word of God.) When you believe the Word of God, you have something solid on which to stand, because faith is based on the knowledge of God's Word. And faith enables you to enter into the grace of God.

Once you've been called by God, it's an irrevocable calling. You may have a call of God on your life and not even know it. But the fact that you don't know what God has called you to do doesn't release you from the charge to do it. Furthermore, it also doesn't release you from the grace God has granted you to accomplish it. You are responsible to find out what God wants you to do.

The reason why God spoke to me about my call in the first place was that I had been spending hours, days and weeks with Him in prayer. I was seeking God. I was spending quality time with Him. That's the atmosphere that creates an ability to hear from God. When you want to hear something from God about His will for your life, begin to spend quality time seeking Him, and He will answer you.

CALLED AND QUALIFIED

You can do anything God tells you to do, because if He calls you, He also qualifies you. If God instructs you to do something, He will give you the grace to do it. God will never ask you to do something you're unable to do. God is fair and just. God is on your side, and He grants His grace to His people. Thank God for His grace!

In Ephesians 3, we see that those who are called to the ministry are given the grace to be in the ministry.

> **That the Gentiles should be fellowheirs, and of
> the same body, and partakers of his promise in
> Christ by the gospel: whereof I was made a minis-
> ter, according to the gift of the grace of God given
> unto me by the effectual working of his power.**
>
> Ephesians 3:6,7

People don't choose the ministry; the ministry chooses them. In other words, a person should not decide to enter the ministry because he has a nice voice and someone said he was handsome! God must call him. Just because a person may look good or have leadership qualities, that doesn't automatically qualify him or her as one called to the ministry. Personality traits have nothing to do with it. There are many good-talking, good-looking people who believe they ought to be in the ministry because their grandmother, their mother or someone else told them that they ought to be a preacher. If people like that go into the ministry for those reasons, they will fall flat on their faces because they weren't called to the ministry. They have no anointing—no grace—to do it.

You shouldn't go into the ministry because you want to; you should go into the ministry because God has called you to do it. And anyone God calls, He gives that person the grace needed to do the job. If they don't get it done, either God didn't call them, or they didn't do what He told them to do. If they had heard from God and did what He said, they would have had the grace to complete the task.

With God's grace, you can do whatever God has told you to do, and if you have the faith to believe for it, you can do it magnificently!

If God tells you, for example, to be a preacher, a teacher, a nurse, a doctor or whatever He has called you to be, He will give you the grace to do that task. It's time to agree with God and begin to praise Him that you can do it! It's time to get up and start walking, talking and acting like you can do it. Because you can!

Many times people will pursue careers in different cities or states, and after they have secured the job there, they will then start looking for a church to attend. That's doing it backwards. What they should do is find a good church to belong to first, and then find a good job. A believer's church home is the central focus that provides spiritual feeding and training from the Word. After they find a local church home, they should then find the job God has for them to do there. By putting spiritual things first, people can then be directed by the Holy Spirit to the right job. It's just a matter of making God the top priority.

The paycheck you get from your job is not the source of your supply. *God* is the source of your supply, and He can get whatever He needs to get to you in any way He wants! As long as you're a faithful tither, you need to stop looking at your job as your source. If your job was your source and something happened that prevented you from working, then you'd be out of business! But God is never out of business. He's never out of wealth. He's never out of supply. He's never

THE GRACE OF GOD

out of whatever you need! He is the One who supplies all your needs according to His riches in glory. (Phil. 4:19.)

When you are where God wants you to be, grace is there as well. Stop saying that you can't do something for whatever reason—that you're too old or young, too black or white, too male or female, too educated or uneducated. Simply decide to do what God wants you to do. There's grace available to you in God's will, and you will succeed when you obey and apply His grace for the task.

As you continue to believe God and walk in faith, grace will grow and be multiplied as you need it. You may start at one level, but as you walk into greater levels of faith, the manifestation of that grace will also increase. Eventually, you will fulfill what God has called you to do—by the grace of God!

Let's look at what can accompany God's grace.

> **Paul, a servant of Jesus Christ, called to be an apostle, separated unto the gospel of God, (which he had promised afore by his prophets in the holy scriptures,) concerning his Son Jesus Christ our Lord, which was made of the seed of David according to the flesh; and declared to be the Son of God with power, according to the spirit of holiness, by the resurrection from the dead: by whom we have received grace and apostleship, for obedience to the faith among all nations, for his name.**
>
> **Romans 1:1-5**

The Rutherford translation says, **We have received favor and apostleship.**[1] First, notice that grace and apostleship go together; favor and apostleship go together. If God has called you to do something, you've been favored by Him to do it. It's an honor to do anything for the kingdom of God. It's an honor, for example, to carry a trash can for the kingdom of God. It's an honor to carry an offering plate for the kingdom of God. It's an honor to do anything God has called you to do, and He will give you the grace to complete the task.

When you begin to operate in grace by faith—by acting on what you believe—God will give you even more grace. In turn, when you have more grace, you can accomplish greater tasks with a greater anointing. It is a cycle that increases in glory.

CHAPTER 3

GRACE AND FAITH: GOD'S UNMERITED GIFTS

God gives His grace abundantly to meet whatever need we may have in life. We know we can freely access this grace by faith, and we can access it every time we need it. Why? Because both grace and faith are gifts from God. A gift is something freely given. We can't earn a gift. All we can do is simply ask for the unlimited, unmerited grace of God, believing that we receive it by faith.

We've already looked at several different definitions of grace, but now let's look at a side of grace that will help you receive all the blessings that God has to give.

GRACE AS THE GENEROSITY OF GOD

Notice how the Bible uses the word *grace* to describe God's generosity.

Having predestinated us unto the adoption of children by Jesus Christ to himself, according to the good pleasure of his will, to the praise of the

glory of his grace, wherein he hath made us accepted in the beloved.

Ephesians 1:5,6

In this passage we see that God adopted us into His fellowship because of His great love and generosity toward us. In the *New Testament in Modern English*, the word *grace* also describes the generosity of God. God is generous! He gave you eternal salvation, the Holy Ghost, healing, righteousness, peace and joy. God is generous toward you. You didn't earn one thing from Him. Every gift God has given to you came freely by His grace and by His generosity. God's generosity is unlimited. And you can have more of this grace—this generosity of God—manifested in your life by faith, by believing that God is generous, that He is the rewarder of those who diligently seek Him! (Heb. 11:6.)

BELIEVING IN GOD THE REWARDER

One of the definitions of the word *rewarder* is one who will give from what he has for his own profit.[1] Another definition of the word *rewarder* is one who will discharge and pay off debts that are due.[2]

God is generous; He will take what He has and pay off what debt you have. But in order to receive that grace, you must believe in the nature of God's generosity. God's grace is His generosity. God has repeatedly demonstrated His generosity to men and women throughout the Bible. He demonstrated His grace toward Abraham, for example, even though Abraham made many mistakes. God declared him righteous because of his faith, and God will show His generosity toward you today. If God did it for them, He will do it for you.

GRACE AS RIGHTEOUSNESS

Let's examine God's grace toward Abraham, looking at the connection between grace and faith.

What shall we say then that Abraham our father, as pertaining to the flesh, hath found? For if Abraham were justified by works, he hath whereof to glory; but not before God. For what saith the scripture? Abraham believed God, and it was counted unto him for righteousness. Now to him that worketh is the reward not reckoned of grace, but of debt.

Romans 4:1-4

According to this passage of Scripture, Abraham was declared righteous by God, not because of what he *did,* but because of what he *believed.* Abraham didn't earn the generosity of God because he did good works. God called Abraham righteous because Abraham had faith. Abraham believed what God said He would do, and it was counted to him as righteousness. Does that mean Abraham was perfect? Of course not. Abraham made mistakes just like we do.

THE RIGHTEOUSNESS OF ABRAHAM

Abraham missed it a few times. Remember when God called Abraham and said, *I want you to go over here; don't take any family with you.* And then the first thing Abraham did was to take his nephew!

Then God said, "I'm going to take you to a place you know not of." That's when Abraham went to Egypt where he said to his wife, "You are so fine and beautiful that they will kill me to have you. So I'm going to lie and tell them you're my sister."

At that point, did Abraham sound like a big man of faith? No, not at all!

Then God came to Abraham and said, *I'm in covenant with you; you know that I'm going to do what I said, because I'm walking through this blood.* (Genesis 15:7-21.) "I'm going to give you a child."

Abraham asked, "How do I know it's going to be so?"

Sarah came to Abraham and said, "I know God said we were going to have a baby, but what God probably meant was that you're going to have a child with somebody else. Why don't you take my beautiful young handmaiden and have sex with her? That's how you're going to get your son."

This "great man of faith" said, "Really? You mean you want me to...? Okay, no problem!" And Abraham hastened! But that wasn't God's plan, and it affected his relationship with God for thirteen years.

So, you see, Abraham was quite a mess at first. He sure didn't earn the grace of God. So, how did he eventually receive it? By faith. Abraham finally chose to believe God, and his faith was counted unto him for righteousness— right-standing with God.

The grace of God is righteousness! And we have access by faith into this grace!

Abraham was a person just like you and me, and if he could access the grace of God by faith, then so can we. We don't always have to struggle to receive anything from God; we must put our faith in God and rely on His grace!

THE RIGHTEOUSNESS OF PAUL

Let's look at another man whom we consider righteous. Paul was a man in the Word of God who accessed God's grace on a continual basis.

> It is not expedient for me doubtless to glory. I will come to visions and revelations of the Lord. I knew a man in Christ above fourteen years ago, (whether in the body, I cannot tell; or whether out of the body, I cannot tell: God knoweth;) such an one caught up to the third heaven. And I knew such a man, (whether in the body, or out of the body, I cannot tell: God knoweth;) how that he was caught up into paradise, and heard unspeakable words, which it is not lawful for a man to utter.

37

> **And lest I should be exalted above measure through the abundance of the revelations, there was given to me a thorn in the flesh, the messenger of Satan to buffet me, lest I should be exalted above measure.**
>
> **2 Corinthians 12:1-4,7**

This verse identifies the controversy surrounding Paul's "thorn in the flesh." Many biblical teachers believe that Paul had some sort of health problem. Some people have even gone so far as to say that Paul's *thorn in the flesh* indicated an eye disease with flowing pus, clubbed feet or a hunched back. How could Paul have preached the healing power of God with pus running out of his eyes, with clubbed feet or with a hunched back? If he himself couldn't see, how could he have said to someone else, "Be healed in the name of Jesus"? How could he have carried out the work God had called him to do with such a deformed body?

The *thorn in the flesh* of 2 Corinthians 12 was not a sickness or a disease. The word *messenger* in verse 7 is translated "angelos" in the Greek.[3] It's found 188 times in Scripture, and 181 times it is translated "angel." The other seven times, the word *messenger* is translated "individual."[4]

Paul said this messenger, this individual, was sent to buffet him. The word *buffet* means continual or repeated blows or strikes—something that kept coming to hit Paul every time he turned around.[5] Paul was talking about a demon spirit who persecuted him everywhere he went. Every time Paul went to Lystra and Iconium, persecution arose. The devil used various people within his influence to come against Paul.

> **For this thing I besought the Lord thrice, that it might depart from me. And he said unto me, My grace is sufficient for thee: for my strength is made perfect in weakness. Most gladly therefore will I rather glory in my infirmities, that the power of Christ may rest upon me.**
>
> 2 Corinthians 12:8,9

Paul went before the Lord and prayed, "Lord, please remove this demon from me." He prayed this not once, not twice, but three times.

The Lord finally spoke to him and said, *Paul, My grace is sufficient for you.*

You see, Paul was a person just like you and me; he sometimes forgot about the grace of God. We have a tendency to put the men of God on pedestals, making them almost untouchable. But these men and women of the Bible were not that much different from us. Paul experienced strife and conflict with brothers; he had arguments with people, just as we do today.

THE RIGHTEOUSNESS OF ELIJAH

There are many others in the Bible who received grace despite their shortcomings. Elijah was one of these men. Elijah was a great prophet of God who called fire down from heaven. How would you like to cause the heavens to open and cause fire to come down, consuming everything in sight?

I'm from Detroit, and I can just imagine what it would be like to call all the Islamic and Buddhist followers together downtown, just as Elijah did when he summoned all the prophets of Baal together.

I would declare, "We are going to find out today whose god is real. Are you up for this?"

They would respond, "Yeah, let's do it!" So we would go to the middle of downtown Detroit and build an altar of sacrifice.

Then I would tell them, "Now, you call on your god, and I'm going to call on mine; whichever one is real will answer by fire."

Well, I'll tell you what would happen: They would call on their gods and do all kinds of things to get a response, but nothing would happen. I would then respond by saying, "Your god must be on vacation; maybe he found a girlfriend and ran off somewhere!"

That was exactly what Elijah did; he called for all the prophets of Baal to join him at Mount Carmel. (1 Kings 18:21-40.) There the prophets of Baal called and called upon their god, yet they received no answer. Then Elijah called on his God and said, "God, You are God of heaven. Let all Israel know that there is a God here in Israel!"

Fire immediately fell from heaven—consuming the entire sacrifice and even licking up the surrounding water, dirt and rocks. Everyone declared, "The Lord—He is God!"

Well, after seeing God consume everything in such a manner, I would have believed He was God too!

Now, you would think that if a man could call fire down from heaven, he would not be afraid of anything or anyone. Yet, when Jezebel sent Elijah a note the next day, saying, "I'm going to take your head tomorrow," Elijah panicked. Instead of saying, "Come on, baby. You want some fire? I'll turn you into a crispy critter," Elijah started running in fear. He ran until he finally fell down under a tree. Then he cried out to God, "God, kill me! Jezebel's going to kill me so You might as well do it now. There's no one left but me, God." (1 Kings 19:10.)

God replied, "What are you doing under that tree?" God then told Elijah what to do. (1 Kings 19:9-18.)

Notice in 1 Kings 19 that one minute Elijah was "up," and the next minute he was down and dejected, just like some of us are. These men and women in the Bible were subject to the same passions you and I experience today.

Paul was no different than Elijah and other men and women of the Bible. Paul said, "God, please get this demon off me. Every time I go somewhere, this persecution comes up, and I get hit in the head with a rock or something. Do something about this, God!" (2 Cor. 12:8.)

GRACE AS THE REVELATION OF THE AUTHORITY OF THE BELIEVER

God's response to Paul reveals another meaning of the word *grace*. When Paul cried out to God, God answered Paul by saying, **My grace is sufficient for thee** (2 Cor. 12:9).

41

What does that tell us about the grace of God? Grace is God's revelation of our authority in Christ. God never asked you to pray and ask Him to do something about the devil. No, God said, **Resist the devil, and he will flee from you** (James 4:7). Jesus said, **All power is given unto me in heaven and in earth.** (Matt. 28:18).

Paul understood what God was trying to say about his own authority on the earth. So Paul jumped right out of doubt and moved into the realm of faith. His faith then accessed God's grace! As soon as God said, *My grace is sufficient,* Paul's faith was activated. He realized that he couldn't do anything in his own strength or ability to prevent the persecution that was coming against him. Instead, he decided to use the authority that Jesus gave him and to believe that the name of Jesus, the blood of Jesus and the Word of God were sufficient to overcome his problem.

GRACE AS THE REVELATION
OF THE WORD OF GOD

A closer look at Paul's life reveals yet another definition of the grace of God.

As long as Paul was complaining about the persecution that seemed to appear everywhere he went, he was not in faith. And as long as he was feeling sorry for himself and as long as he was discouraged, he couldn't access the grace available to him. Grace was available the whole time, but only when Paul moved into the realm of faith was he able to access God's grace.

How was he able to make the switch from discouragement to faith? By speaking God's words out of his mouth. Paul said, **For when I am weak** [in my own self], **then am I strong** [in God] (2 Cor. 12:10). When you speak what the Word of God says about you instead of doubt and unbelief, you gain access to the grace of God.

Another definition of grace is the revelation of the Word. God's Word is the grace of God. Wherever there is revelation of the Word of God, you have the opportunity to act in faith—to believe whatever the Word of God says you can have. First Peter 1:2 says that grace and peace are multiplied through the knowledge of God and of Jesus our Lord. In other words, grace and peace are multiplied through the revelation of God's Word.

When you have a revelation of God's Word, you can stand in the grace of God. Paul received the grace of God, and look what happened to him. By the end of the book of Acts, it says that Paul as a prisoner was living in his own hired house, preaching the gospel to every man, and no man was forbidding him. (Acts 28:30,31.) That was the grace of God!

Paul resisted the demon spirit who was troubling him, and so can you. Satan has no right to be in your house. He has no right to be near your children. He has no right to be around your family. He has no right to be influencing your finances. He has no right to be in your body or touch anything else that belongs to you! God has given you grace—the name of Jesus, the Word of God, the power of the blood and faith—to drive Satan out of your life!

Because of what Jesus did (not because of anything you have done), you have power over the enemy. Remember, Jesus said, **All power is given unto me in heaven and in earth. Go ye therefore...** (Matt. 28:18,19). You have this power when you receive it by faith. There's enough power in you and there's enough power in the name of Jesus to deal with any demon, no matter how big he appears to be in your life.

When I first got saved, I remember going to church and seeing a boy who was demon possessed. He and I were sitting on opposite sides of the choir. He was sitting right behind my wife. Well, one day while we were singing, all of a sudden, that demon rose up in this boy, and he began to carry on and growl. He slammed his head against the wall and then jumped out and ran behind the choir stand. He ran down the stairs and into the middle of the congregation. He kept on running with a contorted look all over his face. People all over the congregation were diving underneath the pews, saying, "That demon's going to get on me!" I thought the same thing, *If it can get on them, it can get on me too!* This continued until someone finally was able to minister to that boy and he was delivered. But back then I was afraid of demons because I didn't realize the authority I had in Christ. I didn't have a revelation of the Word of God in this area.

I remember when I first went to college, a buddy of mine (who happens to be a pastor today) and I were known all over campus, because we witnessed to everyone we could find. In fact, when we would walk down the main hallway, the crowd of students would part just like the Red Sea! Students would get out of the way because they knew we were going to preach to someone.

If a person was walking down the hall, we would stop him and ask, "Do you know Jesus? Are you saved?" He would usually try to walk away from us. But we would continue, "Do you know that you're going to go to hell? You have to get saved!" Unfortunately, we were zealous without knowledge (Prov. 19:2), although our intentions were right.

My friend and I preached to everyone and everything we could find. If it moved, we preached to it! One night at about two or three o'clock in the morning, my buddy received a phone call. As soon as he got off the phone he called me and said, "Get up! We have to go across campus. There's a girl over there who's demon possessed. We're going to cast the devil out of her."

I said, "Okay, I'm game. Let's go." When we got to her dormitory, we went upstairs and heard all kinds of commotion in the hallway. It sounded like furniture being slammed around, and there were people shouting.

When we got into the girl's room, we saw five or six guys trying to subdue her. This was amazing because the girl was small. She was under five feet tall and weighed no more than one hundred pounds. Yet she was throwing full-grown guys up against the wall and across the room. As soon as my buddy saw what was going on, he put his head down, ran and slammed right into her! He knocked her on the floor, put his hands on top of her head and said, "Come out in the name of Jesus!"

I was right behind him. I was right by his shoulder, shouting, "Yeah, come out in Jesus' name!" But that devil didn't come out right away. We were using the name of Jesus that way because we had heard someone else do it, not because we had a personal revelation of the Word for ourselves in that area.

When that demon started talking back, it took us by surprise. A man's voice came out of that tiny girl! It said, "You can't cast me out. Ha, ha, ha." I heard that and took two steps back because I had never seen or heard anything like that before in my life.

My buddy spoke back to that demon and said, "Yeah, you're coming out! You're coming out in the name of Jesus!" I was agreeing with my buddy but from a distance. I wasn't going to get any closer and put my hand within reach of the girl. I thought she might bite it off or something!

To make a long story short, she was delivered before class began that morning. And then she got saved and filled with the Holy Spirit. The grace of God was sufficient, and I give all the credit to God and to my buddy, because they sure didn't get much help from me! But, you see, I didn't know about the authority of the believer as I do now.

It's a good thing we had God's grace to help her back
then. God made up for our shortcomings in our understanding of our authority. Thank God for His spiritual gifts!

God has given you grace. He has given you the name of
Jesus, the Word, the blood and the measure of faith that you
need—the ability to believe in the power of these things.
That is all the grace you need to deal with any devil under
any circumstance! You don't need to be afraid of the devil.
Just tell him to shut up and leave in Jesus' name!

GRACE AS THE MERCY OF GOD

In the Twentieth Century translation, grace is also translated as the mercy of God.[6] The mercy of God is the grace
of God.

> **But the unbelieving Jews stirred up the**
> **Gentiles, and made their minds evil affected**
> **against the brethren. Long time therefore abode**
> **they speaking boldly in the Lord, which gave testi-**
> **mony unto the word of his grace, and granted**
> **signs and wonders to be done by their hands.**
>
> **Acts 14:2,3**

Let's review Romans 4 to remind ourselves what God's
Word says about accessing the grace of God. Romans 4:16
says, **Therefore it is of faith, that it might be by grace....** It
is by faith that we access the grace and the promises of God.

Since the grace of God is manifested through faith, then you must be sure you stand on your faith and utterly depend on it. You must be sure that God's grace is going to be available to you day in and day out. You must be sure to understand that you can't earn grace in order to receive it. The grace of God is based on faith in God's Word, and God's Word never fails.

GRACE AS THE PEACE OF GOD

Notice in the following passage of Scripture that grace is defined as the peace of God.

> **Therefore being justified by faith, we have peace with God through our Lord Jesus Christ: by whom also we have access by faith into this grace wherein we stand, and rejoice in hope of the glory of God.**
>
> **Romans 5:1,2**

The peace of God is ours by faith. But once we've entered into faith we need to stay in faith in order to maintain that peace. How do we stay in faith? Romans 5:2 tells us to rejoice or give praises to God.

Praise is an act of faith that opens the door to God's promises, including the grace of God in your life. Praise will also open the door to miracles in your life. Every believer should praise God in the morning, in the afternoon and in the evening from out of the abundance of his or her heart.

That is how you stay in faith and how you keep yourself from discouragement. When you praise God, you are thanking Him for all that Jesus has done for you. When you praise God, you are unlocking the power of His grace in your life.

THE GRACE OF OUR JESUS CHRIST

Jesus Himself is the grace of God.

For ye know the grace of our Lord Jesus Christ, that, though he was rich, yet for your sakes he became poor, that ye through his poverty might be rich.

2 Corinthians 8:9

The grace of Jesus Christ in this form can be accepted or rejected. You already know that it is possible to reject God. Well, if you can reject God, you can also reject God's grace. You can reject any area of the grace of God any time you want. Furthermore, anything you reject from God, you will not receive in your life. But the good news is that you can choose to receive God's grace in any area of your life by faith. And, according to 2 Corinthians, Jesus Christ—the grace of God—has become poor for our sake so that we might obtain the riches of God!

But this I say, He which soweth sparingly shall reap also sparingly; and he which soweth bountifully shall reap also bountifully. Every

49

man according as he purposeth in his heart, so let
him give; not grudgingly, or of necessity: for God
loveth a cheerful giver. And God is able to make
all grace abound toward you; that ye, always
having all sufficiency in all things, may abound to
every good work.

2 Corinthians 9:6-8

When grace abounds toward you, prosperity also
abounds, and other areas of your life become fully supplied.
With grace you can have a sufficiency in all things. And you
can enjoy this grace—multiplied and abounding in your
life—by faith.

I want you to understand that you can't receive anything from God without faith. When you think that you
have come to a place in God where you are so mature that
you no longer need to study about faith, you have become
deceived. Faith is the key for your access into the all-
important grace of God.

CHAPTER 4

WHAT GRACE CAN DO FOR YOU

G race is God's free gift to His children, and it can bring many benefits in your life. The Word of God reveals many things that the grace of God can do for you. First Peter 1:2 says that grace can grow and be multiplied in your life. Grace can flow out abundantly and be ministered to you. Grace can give you hope and encouragement. The grace of God defends and strengthens you. And every one of us who has accepted Jesus Christ as Savior has been saved by the grace of God through faith!

GRACE SAVES YOU

And [God] hath raised us up together, and made us sit together in heavenly places in Christ Jesus.... For by grace are ye saved through faith; and that not of yourselves: it is the gift of God.

Ephesians 2:6,8

I didn't always know that salvation is a free gift. When I was growing up, I was taught that if at the end of my life, my good works outweighed my bad works, then I would be saved and go to heaven when I died. I was taught that God is the Judge, and He has a scale on which He would weigh my works. If my good works outweighed my bad works, then I'd get into heaven. But if my bad works outweighed my good works, then I would find myself in hell.

That may be what many people believe, but that's not how it works according to the Word of God. If it did work that way, that would mean that I have to earn my salvation. And none of us can do enough good works to earn our way into heaven. We can't wash away our sin. We were born in sin with a sin nature that we cannot overcome on our own. But, thank God, He sent Jesus to handle the sin problem for us.

When I was growing up, I didn't know that I could simply receive salvation by asking Jesus to come into my life and be my Lord. But I'm so glad I found out the truth. I'm so glad I found out that salvation is *received* and not *earned!*

The day I went to the altar to confess Jesus as the Lord of my life, I didn't feel anything physically. I had been expecting some lightning bolt to hit me or at least a feeling of quivers, shakes or something! I was expecting some kind of physical reaction that would verify to me in the natural that I had just become a member of the kingdom of God. But you don't have to feel anything physically or emotionally in order to be saved. The Bible says that when we receive Jesus, we become sons and daughters of God, regardless of our feelings or expectations.

But as many as received him, to them gave he power to become the sons of God, even to them that believe on his name: which were born, not of blood, nor of the will of the flesh, nor of the will of man, but of God. And the Word was made flesh, and dwelt among us, (and we beheld his glory, the glory as of the only begotten of the Father,) full of grace and truth.

John 1:12-14

Jesus, the Living Word, is full of grace—favor, revelation, anointing, generosity and kindness. He is the living representative of the grace of God!

Not only is He full of grace, but He's also full of truth. Grace and truth go together hand in hand. Jesus said in John 17:17, **Thy word is truth.** The world is looking for truth, and it is found in the Word of God.

Let's continue to read in the book of John.

John bare witness of him, and cried, saying, This was he of whom I spake, He that cometh after me is preferred before me: for he was before me. And of His fulness have all we received, and grace for grace.

John 1:15,16

What have we received? We have received all the fullness of His grace. God is not choosing certain people and deciding that He will only give grace to those few. It doesn't work like that. God has provided grace for the entire body of Christ, and His grace can be accessed by anyone.

OUR SIN IN EXCHANGE FOR HIS GRACE

Jesus exchanged what we had, sin, with what He had, His grace. He took upon Himself the sin of the world and gave us access to the grace of God. It was not a fair swap, but I'm so glad He made it! Because of Jesus' sacrifice, we have received all the grace that is available from God Almighty.

According to Ephesians 2:8, we are saved by grace. Well, what does the word *saved* mean? The Greek word for *saved* is *sozo*. The word *sozo* in verse 8 means to be healed.[1] In other words, by grace we have been healed through faith. We don't have to earn our healing by going to church or by doing some other kind of good work, because grace cannot be earned. As I said before, grace is unmerited.

The word *saved* also means preserved as opposed to being destroyed.[2] So, by the grace of God, you have been preserved through your faith in Christ instead of being destroyed by your sin.

To be saved also means to be made whole.[3] Everything that has cost you anything, you will receive restoration for. For example, if you were attacked and lost all of your money, you would receive all of your money back again; this is what it means to be made whole.

Let's look at someone in the Bible who was made whole. Jesus said to the woman with the issue of blood, **Daughter,**

thy faith hath made thee whole (Mark 5:34). He didn't say that she was healed; He said that she was *made whole*. In verse 26, we are told that this woman had spent all that she had to cure her condition and was not any better but had become worse. First she became worse in her body, and then she lost her money. By the time she encountered Jesus, she was both poverty-stricken and sick.

But when she received the anointing on Jesus through her faith, she was made whole. What was Jesus saying when He said that she was "made whole"? Not only was she healed in her body, but she was also promised divine compensation for all the money she had spent on physicians! She accessed the grace of God which ensured she would gain everything back that was stolen from her. If you will access God's grace through faith for your needs to be met, God will do the same thing for you!

The word *saved* also means to be made sound—sound in mind, sound in body and sound in every way. How do you access this soundness? Through your faith. You have access by your faith into the grace of God—into everything that His grace provides.

What does His grace make available to you? Healing is available to you. Preservation is available to you. Wholeness is available to you. Soundness is available to you. In other words, grace provides you with everything you need. You don't have to work for it; you don't have to earn it; you don't even have to sweat for it! All you have to do is believe.

If you examine the word *faith* at its most basic level, what does it mean? Faith can be defined as a belief, persuasion or strong conviction.[4] So, if you can believe God for it, the grace that has already been provided can be yours. The grace of God belongs to you. Inner healing belongs to you. Preservation belongs to you. You aren't going to get these things; they are yours *now!*

GRACE BRINGS ABUNDANCE

You don't have to do anything to receive the grace of God except to simply believe and receive. The pressure is off of you to perform. Receiving the grace of God is not based on works, such as going to church or standing in a healing line or giving a certain amount of money. Many people have even made their "faith" into works by thinking they constantly have to repeat, "I believe I receive. I believe I receive." Their confession actually becomes a matter of works.

No, all you have to do is receive what is already available. And I have good news: There is an abundance of grace available for you!

> Every man according as he purposeth in his heart, so let him give; not grudgingly, or of necessity: for God loveth a cheerful giver. And God is able to make all grace abound toward you; that ye, always having all sufficiency in all things, may abound to every good work.
>
> **2 Corinthians 9:7,8**

Notice the word *all* in verse 8—it means everything! If anything were left out, then it wouldn't be "all." And when something is "abounding toward you," it's coming your way. It's actually leaping your way! All of God's grace is coming your way. It's already jumping toward you.

There's nothing and no one big enough to stand in God's way. There's nothing that the devil can do to circumvent the abounding grace of God. That grace extends to every area of our lives. When we obey God's Word in one area, we may see the results in other areas as well. I'm constantly amazed by how the planting of a seed in one area will produce a harvest in another area. But there are examples of this principle in the Old and New Testaments of the Bible.

In 2 Kings 4, a rich woman gave food to Elisha, the prophet of God, and even built him a prophet's chamber in her home. Elisha came to her and said, "What do you need?"

She said, "I don't need anything."

"Oh, you must need something," he said. "What do you need?"

Elisha's servants responded and said, "She needs a child because her husband is old."

As a result of this rich woman's gift to the prophet of God, she received her heart's true desire—a baby boy. When she gave to Elisha in faith, she opened the door for the grace of God to be poured out in her entire life.

In the New Testament, this principle is demonstrated the same way. All of God's grace is opened up to you by the acts of your faith. Whatever you can believe for that is in line with God's Word, you can receive. The pressure is off of you. You don't have to make something happen. The only thing you have to do is believe, because God has already done the work for you. That's what the grace of God is all about. You have access into that grace by your faith—by your ability to believe.

Let's look what God did through Jesus Christ so that you could enjoy His grace!

> **Nevertheless death reigned from Adam to Moses, even over them that had not sinned after the similitude of Adam's transgression, who is the figure of him that was to come. But not as the offence, so also is the free gift. For if through the offence of one many be dead, much more the grace of God, and the gift by grace, which is by one man, Jesus Christ, hath abounded unto many. And not as it was by one that sinned, so is the gift: for the judgment was by one to condemnation, but the free gift is of many offences unto justification.**
>
> **Romans 5:14-16**

Notice the word *free* in this passage of Scripture. When something is free, you don't have to pay for it. In this context, it means that you don't have to pay anything for the grace of God; you don't have to do anything to receive it except believe.

Because Adam sinned, many people died. Sin is powerful enough to kill people! But there is something that is stronger than death and sin. The Bible says that the free gift of God's grace has been made abundant to many by the one man, Jesus Christ. God's grace is stronger than sin.

Adam's sin in the Garden of Eden allowed death to take charge, reigning as a king in this world. Death reigned before Christ, but death has been replace by someone else who now reigns over death—Jesus Christ the Savior, the Anointed One. And if we are in Christ, we are reigning in life, too!

Because of Jesus Christ, everyone can receive grace. You don't have to work, sweat or strain for it. You can receive God's abundance of grace and reign as a king in this life!

For if because of one man's trespass (lapse, offense) death reigned through that one, much more surely will those who receive [God's] overflowing grace (unmerited favor) and the free gift of righteousness (putting them into right standing with Himself) reign as kings in life through the One, Jesus Christ, the Messiah, the Anointed One.

Romans 5:17 AMP

Jesus is the Anointed One, and His anointing, His overflowing grace, has been given to you so that you can reign as a king in this life! What do kings do when they reign? They make decrees. Kings say, "Move," and people move! Kings say, "Come to me," and people come to them! Kings say, "Let it be done," and it is done! You can decree something and see it come to pass if it is based on God's Word and spoken from a right spirit.

I was talking with a man in the barber shop. He was telling me about a certain physical challenge that he was having with his body. I told him, "It's good that we have medical doctors. But don't continually repeat what you've been told by the doctors. Instead, talk about what you want God to do for you." In other words, I was telling him not to rehearse his problem, but that he could decree his body to be healed instead of sick.

I'm not saying that sickness, disease and poverty don't exist. I'm just saying that I don't give them more credit than they deserve. I don't spend all of my time talking about them. I would rather talk about what God said. Faith comes by hearing the Word of God. (Rom. 10:17.) And faith is what gives you access into God's grace. You can reign as a king in this life over sickness, disease and poverty when you receive the grace of God through your faith.

God's rest is available for you. The place of rest is the place of faith. You can reign in life without effort—without struggling with your faith. All you have to do is relax and rest in God and believe that the grace of God is already available for you in whatever area you need it—in your body, your finances, your family or any other area!

Wherever you go and whatever you do, the grace of God is abounding toward you; it's already hopping toward you!

And there is always more grace available. God is a God of abundance. He is the God who gives good measure, pressed down, shaken together and running over. (Luke 6:38.) And all you have to do to receive God's grace is believe! Faith gives you access into the grace of God.

GRACE STRENGTHENS YOU

God's grace not only saves you and brings you abundance, but it strengthens you as well. Let's look at a Scripture that will help you understand how strength can come from the grace of God.

Thou therefore, my son, be strong in the grace that is in Christ Jesus.

2 Timothy 2:1

Paul is writing to a young preacher named Timothy. And what Paul is telling Timothy, he's telling you too. Paul didn't tell Timothy to be strong in *himself;* he told Timothy to be strong in grace—in the help and spiritual blessing of the Lord Jesus Christ.

What does it mean to be strong in grace? It means that we don't have to work for things in our own strength because Jesus already purchased all we could ever need when He died and rose again. Instead, we can be strong in Christ—in the fact that He has already provided whatever we may need in this life.

As I said before, there is grace, and therefore strength, for whatever you need to do—particularly if God told you to do something for His kingdom. For example, if the Lord told you to go into the ministry, there would be an abundance of grace and strength to do that. If God told you to go back to your husband instead of divorcing him, there would be an abundance of grace and strength to do that. Whatever God tells you to do, you can do, because there is an abundance of grace that comes along with doing His will.

GRACE DEFENDS YOU

We've seen that grace saves you, causes you to abound and strengthens you, but now let's look at how grace defends you.

For the grace of God that bringeth salvation hath appeared to all men.

Titus 2:11

In this verse, the word *salvation* in the Greek means "defense."[5] This means that the grace of God will defend you. God's grace will protect you and keep you safe against any attack of the enemy.

Every one of these vital meanings of grace is designed to help each member of the body of Christ. All we need to do is tap into God's provision to receive the grace He has for us. That's where faith comes in. As we have already seen, we can access God's grace through faith, but there's an additional factor to consider—the love factor.

LOVE: THE LINK FROM FAITH TO GRACE

First Timothy 1:14 says, **And the grace of our Lord was exceeding abundant with faith and love which is in Christ Jesus.** Notice that Paul mentions faith and love together. Galatians 5:6 says that faith works by love. If you are not walking in love, your faith is not going to be effective. However, the good news is that you *can* walk in love because of God's love for you.

Sometimes it is easier to walk in love than at other times, but you have to walk in love regardless of your feelings. Faith and love must cooperate to produce a result, and if you are involved in strife with someone, your faith will not be as effective as it could be. You may think someone deserves to be punched in the mouth, but you must walk in love regardless of what you think.

In the gospel of Matthew, Jesus talked about "turning the other cheek." (Matt. 5:39.) But He didn't mean that if someone hits you, you should let him hit you again. That's not what Jesus was talking about. Jesus was operating in such a great love for people that grace—God's anointing—became strong enough within Him to overcome hostility from others. The grace of God was what defended Jesus.

In the gospel of Luke, Jesus stood up in the temple and turned to where it is written,

> **The Spirit of the Lord is upon me, because He hath anointed me to preach the gospel to the poor; he hath sent me to heal the brokenhearted,**

to preach deliverance to the captives, and recovering of sight to the blind, to set at liberty them that are bruised, to preach the acceptable year of the Lord.... This day is this scripture fulfilled in your ears.

Luke 4:18,19,21

When Jesus finished speaking, the people looked at Him and became angry because they realized what He was saying. They became so angry that they took Jesus to the edge of the city to throw Him over a cliff. But the Bible says Jesus walked right through them, escaping danger. Not only could the crowd not touch Him, they couldn't even find Him! The grace of God defended Jesus! (Luke 4:28-30.)

God loves us so much that He gave us faith so that we can have access to everything He has for us. He gave us faith so that we can have access to everything that His grace promises us! And God didn't just give some people faith and leave others out. No, He loves each of us the same, giving all of us the same ability to believe! Within every person is a portion of the faith of God. And that faith of God accesses His grace.

GRACE ENCOURAGES YOU

Isn't God's grace wonderful? Look at all of its benefits! God not only gave you salvation, abundance, strength and a strong defense, but His grace offers you hope, consolation and encouragement.

**Now our Lord Jesus Christ himself, and God,
even our Father, which hath loved us, and hath
given us everlasting consolation and good hope
through grace, comfort your hearts.**

2 Thessalonians 2:16,17

The word *consolation* means encouragement.[6] God's grace
is God's encouragement!

The Word of God is one of the best places to find
encouragement. No other source will encourage you like the
Word. For example, when you watch a television show, you
may be left feeling discouraged by the end of the program.
When you open the newspaper, you may not walk away
with hope. There's a lot of bad news in the newspaper. But
when you open God's Word, you'll find hope and encouragement every time, regardless of what the television or the
newspapers say.

When you are feeling down and depressed, you don't
need to pick up a phone and call a friend. Instead, begin
reading God's Word, and He will encourage you. Start
praying when you feel down, and the Holy Spirit will
encourage you. The grace of God will lift you up, because it
is the consolation of God.

GRACE MINISTERS TO YOU

We know that grace saves you, causes you to abound,
strengthens you, defends you and encourages you. But did
you know that grace also ministers to you?

Let no corrupt communication proceed out of your mouth, but that which is good to the use of edifying, that it may minister grace unto the hearers.

Ephesians 4:29

The grace of God can be ministered to you. And you can minister grace by the *words* you say to other people. The manifestation of grace can show up in the life of a person because of what you say to him or her. That's why you need to watch what you say, because you can minister either grace and help or death and corruption to a person, depending on what you say.

Proverbs 18:21 says, **Death and life are in the power of the tongue.** As your mother used to tell you, if you don't have something good to say, don't say anything at all. Your words have an effect on your life and the lives of others around you. They can either be a great blessing or a great curse, but you have the power to determine which they will be.

CHAPTER 5

SHARED GRACE

I thank my God upon every remembrance of you, always in every prayer of mine for you all making request with joy, for your fellowship in the gospel from the first day until now; being confident of this very thing, that he which hath begun a good work in you will perform it until the day of Jesus Christ: even as it is meet for me [Paul] to think this of you all, because I have you in my heart; inasmuch as both in my bonds, and in the defence and confirmation of the gospel, ye all are partakers [sharers] of my grace.

Philippians 1:3-7

Paul said that the grace of God can be shared. Notice that in Philippians 1:5, Paul is thanking the saints at Philippi for their fellowship. The word *fellowship* in the Greek means partnership—two people joining together to accomplish something bigger than what they could do individually.[1] Paul is thanking them for their gifts which allowed him to minister the Word of God. Paul tells them that because they had given him their offerings, the anointing, or grace, that was on him would be accessible to them as well. In other words, the church at Philippi actually shared in the grace given to Paul because of their gifts.

Isn't it interesting to learn that someone else's anointing, or grace, can be can be shared with you by your giving? When two or more people share in a godly anointing, it's called a spiritual partnership. And spiritual partnerships are very important to the study of grace.

THE PLACE OF PRAYER IN PARTNERSHIP

Not only can grace be shared through acts of giving, but it can also be shared through acts of prayer. Paul said, **For I know that this shall turn to my salvation** [deliverance] **through your prayer, and the supply of the Spirit of Jesus Christ** (Phil. 1:19). Paul was dealing with some real tests and trials. He had experienced many difficult obstacles as he was carrying out the call of God on his life.

But in the midst of these difficulties, Paul said, "I know I will succeed, and I know that what I am dealing with will turn to my advantage because of your prayers in the Holy Spirit." His spiritual partnership with the church of Philippi was strengthened by prayer and was able to help him in his times of trouble.

If you say you are a partner in a particular ministry, then the first thing you ought to be doing is praying for that ministry. Prayer is not something you should do religiously. Prayer should come from the heart.

When some people say, "I'll pray for you," they don't really mean it. They may just be saying it to be nice. However, you will find others who will pray in partnership with you, finding out what God's Word says about your situation and praying the Word over you. These are true prayer partners who will share in the grace given to your ministry.

True prayer partners will take the time to join in the spirit with you, knowing that their prayers will support and protect you. Prayer partners are vital because when God's children present their needs to Him, He intervenes on their behalf, turning around any situation for good.

Paul essentially said, "I know I will be all right. I know my situation will turn out well. I know I will be delivered because of your prayers. You are my partners; we are working together." (Phil. 1:19.) Paul was exercising his faith and allowing grace to enter in.

No one can accomplish the will of God by himself. God does not expect one man or woman to be a "superstar" in the church. One minister cannot do everything alone. It is true that not everyone is called to be an apostle, prophet, evangelist, pastor or teacher; but those who are called in these areas cannot go very far without your prayers. Ministers of the gospel must have spiritual partners to release the anointing and the grace in their lives to do what God requires of them.

If you are not receiving everything that you should from a ministry, maybe you should begin a spiritual partnership by praying for them. If you are expecting to receive revelation for yourself from a certain ministry, then you should also be praying for that ministry. There's a sharing of grace that comes when you pray in partnership with a ministry. And as a believer, you have a responsibility to become involved in the partnerships God directs you to.

Did the apostle Paul need prayer partners? Yes! He tells us so in Ephesians 6:19-20.

> **And [pray] for me [Paul], that utterance may be given unto me, that I may open my mouth boldly, to make known the mystery of the gospel, for which I am an ambassador in bonds: that therein I may speak boldly, as I ought to speak.**

In other words, Paul said, "I can't preach the gospel the way I am supposed to unless you enter into partnership with me and pray for me." Paul's boldness was made possible by the prayer support he received from his partners in Ephesus. Paul benefited from this support, and the Ephesians benefited by sharing in Paul's grace.

AN OLD TESTAMENT EXAMPLE OF SHARED GRACE

Let's look at an Old Testament example of a partnership in which grace is shared. First Samuel 30 describes an event where every woman and child of Israel was taken prisoner, and many villages were burned. David, who was fighting against the aggressors, gathered together his men, and they set off on a "forced march" to avenge themselves. A forced march is a march in which soldiers carry all their equipment

as fast as they can and as far as they can in order to be
prepared to fight at any time.

As David's men approached the enemy, two hundred
among them became too tired to go any farther. So David
told them to stay behind to watch the camp. The remaining
four hundred men went out and fought the battle while the
others guarded the supplies. The fighting men emerged
victorious, taking back all the women and children and the
spoil that the enemy had stolen.

Once David's army was reunited, the four hundred men
who had gone out to fight came back saying, "Because the
other two hundred men did not go with us, we will not give
them any of the spoil." (1 Sam. 30:22.) But David replied,
"Everyone receives the same reward." (vv. 23,24.) He treated
each person's job as equally important. A spiritual partnership operates the same way. For example, you may not be
the one in the pulpit, but if you're praying for or giving
tithes and offerings to the person who is in the pulpit, then
you will receive the same reward. When that minister leads
people to Christ, then, as their partner, you will share in that
"spoil." That's the shared grace that comes from being in a
spiritual partnership. You can share in the grace given to a
ministry by being faithful behind the scenes, and God will
bless you for it.

EACH MEMBER IN A PARTNERSHIP IS IMPORTANT

In God's system, everyone involved in a spiritual
partnership is important. Those who park the cars, clean the

restrooms, wash the windows or handle the offerings in the church will ultimately receive the same reward as the person speaking in the pulpit. God treats each member of the partnership fairly. He supplies grace to each member for his or her particular task and rewards each of them equally.

SHARING THE PROPHET'S ANOINTING

Let's look at another example of partnership in the Word of God.

> **And it fell on a day, that Elisha passed to Shunem, where was a great woman; and she constrained him to eat bread. And so it was, that as oft as he passed by, he turned in thither to eat bread.**
>
> **2 Kings 4:8**

This great woman, a Shunammite woman, "constrained" Elisha. In other words, she told him that if he came to town, she and her husband would take care of him. She entered into a partnership with Elisha and became eligible to receive the same anointing that was on Elisha's life. She was not the prophet, yet she shared in the prophet's reward. The grace on Elisha's life transferred to her, and she received a blessing because of her partnership with Elisha.

The Shunammite woman built a prophet's chamber for Elisha; in this case, it was an additional room that served as a bedroom for Elisha. (2 Kings 4:9,10.) However, in 2 Kings 4:14, we learn that the Shunammite woman had been unable to bear a child, and she and her husband had reached old age. Elisha approached the woman and said, **About this season, according to the time of life, thou shalt embrace a son** (v. 16). Now, the woman did not have faith for this, but Elisha did. Because of the partnership that she had with Elisha, the anointing fell on her husband; she was able to share in the grace that was on Elisha and conceive a son.

Just as the Shunammite woman shared in the anointing of Elisha, so you can share in someone else's anointing. For example, you can sow your money, your time or your prayers into a ministry and share in the anointing, or grace, that is on that minister. Because of my spiritual partnership with Kenneth E. Hagin, I have received a part of the grace that has been on his ministry for fifty years. And as God continues to anoint him, I will continue to share in that anointing.

The same thing can happen for you. If the minister with whom you are sharing a spiritual partnership has favor, then you will have favor. If he is blessed, then you will be blessed. You have a right to these rewards, because you have entered into a partnership with him and his rewards are your rewards as well.

God will first call a minister and then give him the anointing and the ability to do things he cannot do on his own. God will then call others to help and support that minister in the work God has called him to do. The partnership between these two parties can accomplish more than what either could have done individually, and as a result, God's work can be done in the earth.

EXPECT TO RECEIVE

More than twenty years ago, I went to a Kenneth E. Hagin meeting for the first time. I had been reading his books and listening to him on the radio. When I found out that he was coming to Detroit, I was so eager to hear him preach the Word that I arrived at the meeting two hours before the doors even opened. There was no one there yet but me, and I wanted a seat right in front of the prophet of God. When the doors finally opened and people rushed forward, I was able to get a seat in the front row, right below the pulpit.

During the meeting, I heard Brother Hagin say something I had never heard a minister say before. He spoke about how God had called and anointed him to minister healing to the sick. Then he said, "If you will believe that God sent me, you can draw on that gift and receive your healing."

Now, the Word of God says that if you believe His prophets, you will prosper. (2 Chron. 20:20.) I didn't have a full understanding of that at the time. But over the years, I've found out that there is a grace on Brother Hagin, and that grace is to stand in the office of a prophet. There are some people who call themselves prophets but who are not. Kenneth Hagin is a true prophet, because he has the gifts and anointing to back it up. And the grace of God that is on him can be accessed by faith and by expectation.

If you come to a service and say, "Well, I don't know what's going to happen, but I hope I receive something from God," you probably won't receive anything. If you want a manifestation of God's grace in your life, you must expect to receive it.

There are some places where I preach and the people are so ready to receive from God, I can feel it. They have come with the attitude, "We're going to receive everything you've got!" They draw on me like a magnet. After I have preached for two hours, they're still saying, "Don't stop!" These people are sharing in the grace that's on me.

Remember that grace is accessed through faith. You must expect to receive. That's how you access the grace of God on another person's life. You can get in on another man or woman's anointing through your expectations. You can access that grace, that anointing, by faith!

CHAPTER 6

THE PRICE
OF GRACE

The grace of God you received when you were born again came with a huge price! Jesus paid the price so you could walk in the freedom of grace through your faith. We could not have paid it ourselves—Jesus had to pay it for us. There was nothing we could do to cleanse ourselves of sin and receive the righteousness of God.

OUR SIN FOR HIS GRACE

Only one person, Jesus Christ, was qualified to pay the price for our salvation. It required One without any sin who could stand in our place. God sent Jesus to the earth to take our place—to become sin for us so that we could receive the grace of God! A great swap took place. Jesus took our sin and gave us His grace. It wasn't a fair trade—our sin for God's grace—but we can receive it nevertheless!

But we see Jesus, who was made a little lower than the angels for the suffering of death, crowned

**with glory and honour; that he by the grace of
God should taste death for every man.**

Hebrews 2:9

You will find there are people who have not received God's grace and are still trying to work for their salvation. I used to be one of those people because I didn't know any better. I wasn't taught the truth about grace at the churches I attended, because the preachers at those churches didn't know any better themselves. So, I thought my salvation was based on good works—that if my good works outweighed my bad works when I died—I would make it into heaven "by the skin of my teeth"!

I remember the day I went to the altar to confess Jesus Christ as my Lord and Savior. Before I got back to my seat, the devil said to me, *You aren't saved. You didn't roll on the floor like those other people and cry.* It was true; I hadn't rolled on the floor, crying. In fact, I didn't feel anything when I got saved.

The devil said, *You're not saved; you haven't done any of the things these other people are doing.* Then he brought an evil thought to my mind and suggested, *If you were really saved, you wouldn't have had that nasty thought.*

I thought to myself, *I must not be saved.* The next Sunday I went right back to the altar and got saved all over again. When I went back home, the devil said to me again, *You aren't saved.*

The next Sunday I went back to the altar again. It became a vicious circle.

Soon after, I was walking in a park, and I found a little tract about the grace of God. It happened to be lying on a park bench. When I picked it up and read it, I discovered it was talking about salvation. This tract compared a train's engine to the Word of God. The middle car was compared to faith and the caboose to feelings. God's Word is what should be in control, and our faith and our feelings should line up with what the Word says. That little analogy helped me understand that all I had to do was believe what God said. I didn't have to feel anything! I got mad at the devil and said, "You lied to me; I am saved!"

I did the same thing when I was filled with the Holy Spirit. I was taught that you had to tarry for the Holy Spirit—that you had to wait on God for some time before you received it. Some people told me to say, "Thank You, Jesus," over and over and that would help me receive the Holy Spirit. Others told me to "hold on," while others said, "Let loose!"

None of these things helped me, and so I "tarried" for the Holy Spirit for a year and four months! But I wasn't going to quit. Everyone else had quit and gone home. But I said, "I'm going to receive the Holy Spirit; this experience belongs to me. I don't know what I have to do, but I'm going to find out. I'm going to keep doing all I know to do, and one day I'm going to get it."

I had heard that some people had tarried for the Holy Spirit for ten, twenty and even thirty years. But I decided that if I had to tarry for the Holy Spirit for fifty years, I was going to do it! I wasn't going to leave this planet without the baptism in the Holy Spirit!

I thought I had to work to receive the Holy Spirit. But then one day I was in my parents' basement reading the Bible, and I came to Luke 11:13: **If ye then, being evil, know how to give good gifts unto your children: how much more shall your heavenly Father give the Holy Spirit to them that ask him?** I realized that all I had to do was ask God for the Holy Spirit! Then I read in the gospel of Mark about how to pray and ask God for this free gift.

> **Therefore I say unto you, What things soever ye desire, when ye pray, believe that ye receive them, and ye shall have them.**
>
> **Mark 11:24**

I prayed, "Father, Your Word says that if I ask You for the Holy Spirit, You will give Him to me. In the name of Jesus, I ask You for the baptism in the Holy Spirit, and I thank You. I believe I receive Him now."

Then, I spoke to the Holy Spirit and said, "Holy Spirit who's on the inside of me now, give me utterance that I may speak in other tongues in Jesus' name." Immediately, I began speaking in tongues. I didn't have to work for it. All I had to do was receive it.

So where does this idea of "tarrying" come from? People have misinterpreted Luke 24:49, where Jesus says to "tarry in Jerusalem until you are endued with power from on high." Notice that Jesus said to "tarry in Jerusalem." Jesus was speaking to His disciples, telling them to wait in the Upper Room in Jerusalem until the Holy Spirit arrived on the Day of Pentecost. But today the Holy Spirit is already here! You don't have to tarry or wait for Him. He is already here on the earth!

Now, there are some of you today who are dealing with the same issue of tarrying. Some of you may be tarrying for your healing. You may not realize that you're doing it, but you're trying to work for your healing. You may think, *If I just do this, I'll get healed,* or *God ought to heal me because I'm the most faithful person in the church. I pay my tithes, and I ought to get my healing.* But the grace of God is not based on your good works; the grace of God can only be received by faith!

You don't have to build your faith up until you get to the place where you can believe that you are healed. Healing is something that has already been paid for. The stripes that Jesus received on His back were for you. He received all types of sickness on His back. You don't have to convince God to heal you. All you have to do is tap into the grace of God and believe that you receive your healing.

Satan will tell you that you can't receive your healing because your faith is not as great as someone else's faith. But you don't have to pay for your healing by having a great deal of faith. You are already a faith person. You have already received the God-kind of faith that you need when you were born again.

Others are dealing with the same issue of tarrying in the area of finances. They think, *I gave my tithe, so I ought to be receiving the money I need right now.* But that's not the way it works. You cannot earn anything from God. You access the grace of God by faith for any area of your life by simply believing what God said. For example, God said in 2 Corinthians 9:6 that if you give a little, you will receive a little in return. On the other hand, if you give much, you will receive much. That is the principle of seedtime and harvest.

People will do all kinds of crazy things with money just because they saw someone else do it in faith. They will run and throw money on the altar because they saw someone else do it—not because the Holy Spirit led them to do it. Instead of being prompted by the Holy Spirit to give, people sometimes follow others' examples because it becomes a fad, not because they are led of God.

You cannot limit the Holy Spirit. God does things in many different ways. One time He might have you throw your offering on the altar at church, and the next time He might have you go down the street and give it to someone in person. If you try to put God in a box, you will probably miss the leading of the Holy Spirit. Be open to God and do whatever He wants you to do, because His grace is sufficient for you. God will give you whatever you need if you'll just believe Him!

You can believe God, because the price has already been paid. Jesus tasted death so that you could operate in the grace of God. The price has already been paid for you to walk in grace, in favor, in the power of the Holy Spirit, in the blessings of God, in help, in mercy, in lovingkindness, in your calling, in generosity, in righteousness, in revelation, in healing, in preservation, in holiness, in soundness and in financial provision. God has already paid the price for all these things to be yours!

You don't have to pay any price whatsoever. These things are free to you, and there is no limit to receiving them! In the world, if something is offered to you free of charge, there is usually a limit as to how much you can take. But God doesn't have any limits. You can take as much as you can carry! You can take as much as you can believe Him for! To believe means to simply trust God—accepting what He said in His Word as the truth.

So, where does this free grace come from? Let's look at the Word to find out.

Grace be unto you, and peace, from God our Father, and from the Lord Jesus Christ.

1 Corinthians 1:3

For the law was given by Moses, but grace and truth came by Jesus Christ.

John 1:17

Grace comes from God and His Son, Jesus. Jesus is full of the grace and truth of God, and those of you who have received Jesus into your life have received this grace and truth. If you're a Christian, the grace and truth of God has driven out the sin and darkness in your life and has made you a new creature in Christ. (2 Cor. 5:17.) As a believer, you've already received the grace of God with salvation.

So, why should it be difficult to receive grace in the area of healing or your finances? You can receive the grace of God in *any* area of your life, because grace comes from Jesus, and Jesus lives inside you! You don't have to work for it. You don't have to run after it. You already have His grace as a born-again child of God!

When you don't have to work for something, then you can operate in joy and peace. You can rejoice that you have everything you need by the grace of God! Just rest in God's grace and thank Him for it, because it's already yours.

CHAPTER 7

YOU CAN STOP THE GRACE

As we've already seen in God's Word, the grace of God is received by faith. (Rom. 5:2.) Therefore, if you're trying to receive grace by anything other than faith, it can have a hindering effect. Anything else that you do to receive the grace of God can actually prevent God's grace from flowing in your life. Let's look at some things that may stop the grace of God from coming to you.

WORKS OF THE FLESH

When we try to sidestep the grace of God by using our own resources, we short-circuit our blessing, rendering His grace meaningless in our lives. Striving in our fleshly strength to receive grace will not work. Let's see what the Word says about trying to earn grace.

> So too at the present time there is a remnant (a small believing minority), selected (chosen) by grace (by God's unmerited favor and graciousness). But if it is by grace (His unmerited favor and

graciousness), it is no longer conditioned on works or anything men have done. Otherwise, grace would no longer be grace [it would be meaningless].

Romans 11:5,6 AMP

Grace is a gift from God that you received when you were called to come into fellowship with Him. When God made you His precious child, He gave you His grace. You didn't earn it.

Notice verse 6 says that if it is by grace, then it is no longer by works. You can't operate in grace and works at the same time. You can actually cancel out the grace of God when you try to earn grace in your own strength. So, instead of living by your works, live by your faith and receive the grace of God into your life.

I am crucified with Christ: nevertheless I live; yet not I, but Christ liveth in me: and the life which I now live in the flesh I live by the faith of the Son of God, who loved me, and gave himself for me. I do not frustrate the grace of God: for if righteousness come by the law, then Christ is dead in vain.

Galatians 2:20,21

As a believer you can say, "I live by faith, so I live by the grace of God. I don't live by works; I live by faith in the Son of God who loves me and gave Himself for me." You can't receive God's grace by both faith and works.

Now I'm not saying that it's wrong to work for God. Paul said, **I also labour, striving according to his working, which worketh in me mightily** (Col. 1:29). Paul could have said, "I work hard by the grace of God." But Paul wasn't working in the flesh, by his own strength and ability. Paul fulfilled his calling in cooperation with the grace of God.

TAPPING INTO THE LIMITLESS GRACE OF GOD

If you're going to live by works, then your works must be able to produce whatever you need in life. But if you're going to live according to your own resources, then you're going to limit the grace you could otherwise receive from God. However, if you choose to live by grace, then by faith, there are no limits to your resources. God's resources are limitless!

There is an abundance of grace available to you. You will never run out of the grace you need with God as your source. You can't run out of grace for healing. You can't run out of grace for finances. You can't run out of grace for joy. You can't run out of grace for anything in God! However, you can create obstacles to God's grace by trying to do everything yourself.

The Israelites were a group of people who stopped believing God and began doing things themselves. And that's what got Israel in trouble. Before they entered the Promised Land, Israel began looking at the giants. Ten of their spies went over into the Promised Land and saw the sons of Anak—giants in the region. The Israelites began considering what they could do in their own strength.

Compared to the giants, they were like grasshoppers. They began to murmur and complain saying, "God brought us out here to kill us." Their unbelief kindled God's anger. He said, *I'm tired of this group. Nobody else is going over into the Promised Land!*

However, there were two among them, Joshua and Caleb, who saw the same giants, but they had different thoughts. Joshua said, "Hey Caleb, see those giants over there? They're dead meat! They're road-kill!" (Num. 13,14.)

What was the difference between Joshua and Caleb and the rest of the Israelites? Joshua and Caleb operated in faith, believing that if God had called them to go to the Promised Land, they were going to make it. But the rest of the Israelites had shifted their focus onto trying to determine if they could do it by themselves. When they found out they couldn't, they began griping about it. And that's when they lost their grace to overcome.

The only two out of that group who eventually made it into the Promised Land were Joshua and Caleb, the men who operated by faith in what God said. The rest of the Israelites never made it in, because they forgot what God had promised and what He had done for them in the past. They forgot how God brought them out of Egypt with a strong hand and their miraculous rescue at the Red Sea. They forgot how God gave them favor even before they left Egypt, receiving money from the Egyptians just before they were delivered! They chose not to look at any of those victories. And by doing that, they actually wasted the grace of God.

**We then, as workers together with him,
beseech you also that ye receive not the grace of
God in vain.**

2 Corinthians 6:1

How do you receive the grace of God in vain? You waste God's grace when you become impatient and try to make things happen yourself. You've got to relax and just "be cool." Take on an attitude of praise. Praise is an expression of faith. Whenever you feel the temptation to start doing things in your own strength, begin praising God. Don't waste His grace.

To move yourself over into faith, you can praise God by saying, "I want to thank You, Father, that You're bigger than the giant I'm facing. You're bigger than my marriage problems. You're bigger than my business problems. You're bigger than my bank account. You're bigger than my employer. You're bigger than whatever I'm dealing with. You've already made a way of deliverance, and I just want to thank You. I just want to praise You. I want to glorify You."

You can stay in faith and out of works by remembering how good God is. Remember that it's not the size of your problem; it's the size of God's grace. And the grace of God is bigger than your problem. There is no match for the grace of God!

DON'T LET THE DEVIL DEPRIVE YOU

Now, Satan will attempt to deprive you of what is already yours. He will try to discourage your faith and move you into a works mentality. He understands what belongs to you because of who you are in Christ. The devil understands that you have authority over him in the name of Jesus. Satan doesn't have any authority over you. He may have some power in this world, but he doesn't have one bit of authority over you. When he attempts to sabotage you, he's doing so illegally. Jesus took care of that problem on the cross. Now, we may make mistakes, but we can get right back into God's grace.

How many times have you made a mistake? Many times, I'm sure! But God has so much grace, mercy and favor for you that's not even available to His angels. You are someone special to God Almighty. You don't have to work for anything from God. God has already given it all to you. It's already yours, so just receive what's available to you. Just receive what God has already offered you.

Every day you should praise God, thanking Him for the grace available to you. When you begin to praise Him, you'll find words of faith coming from your mouth, and words of doubt will depart. You'll find that the power of God—His grace, help, healing and joy—will manifest itself in the midst of your praises.

When Satan tries to deprive you of what is yours, just claim what belongs to you. Speak it out of your mouth. Don't let the devil rob you of what is already yours. Instead praise God because He has already anticipated your needs for every day of your life. You're an overcomer because the Lord is with you everywhere you go. In His grace and goodness, He has opened the door of blessing and favor for you. It's time to stop working for it, and it's time to start praising Him for it. Whatever you need is already taken care of.

If you will take yourself out of the way and stop trying to earn the blessings of God, you'll be able to freely receive God's grace in your life. Begin praising Him and speaking words of faith. Then simply rest in the blessings of God.

WORKS OF FAITH PRODUCE THE GOD-KIND OF RESULTS

There is a difference between works of the flesh and works of faith, as illustrated in the following passage.

What doth it profit, my brethren, though a man say he hath faith, and have not works? can faith save him? If a brother or sister be naked, and destitute of daily food, and one of you say unto them, Depart in peace, be ye warmed and filled; notwithstanding ye give them not those things which are needful to the body; what doth it profit? Even so faith, if it hath not works, is dead, being alone. Yea, a man may say, Thou hast faith, and I have works: shew me thy faith without thy works, and I will shew thee my faith by my works.

James 2:14-18

This passage is talking about works of faith. James says that as a man or woman of faith, you shouldn't just say, "Be blessed" to your brother who has no food when, all the while, you have a whole freezer full. You shouldn't just say to him, "Well, praise God. I'm praying for you. God will take care of it."

No, that's not what James is saying at all! He says you should put some walk behind your talk. You should go to your freezer, take out food and give it to your brother in need. That's ministering the grace of God to someone.

Someone might say, "Suppose my hungry brother comes back every week? There are people like that, you know." The Word of God talks about those people too. It says that a person like that is out of order. And if they continue taking advantage of another person's generosity, then the Bible says they should be treated like an unbeliever. (2 Thess. 3:10,11,14.) No one should just be living off of someone else's charity.

If I knew a brother or sister who needed food, I would certainly help them. But my help wouldn't come just in the way you might think. Not only would I give them food, but I would also tell them what to do so that they wouldn't always need to come back to me for more food. And then I would expect them to practice what I taught.

Sometimes after you've helped someone, he may think all he has to do is to keep coming back for your help. Perhaps you think that by helping him you're walking in love. But, no, that other person needs to take responsibility for himself instead of trying to get you to take responsibility for him.

Let's read on in James to see how a man of God implemented works of faith in his life.

> Was not Abraham our father justified by works,
> when he had offered Isaac his son upon the altar?
> Seest thou how faith wrought with his works, and
> by works was faith made perfect? And the scripture
> was fulfilled which saith, Abraham believed God,
> and it was imputed unto him for righteousness:
> and he was called the Friend of God. Ye see then
> how that by works a man is justified, and not by
> faith only.
>
> James 2:21-24

Abraham had faith, but his faith was justified by his works. He believed God. God told him to take his only son, Isaac, up to a mountain and offer him as a burnt sacrifice to the Lord. Abraham's work of faith was not only to believe God, but also to obey—to act on what God said. Abraham did what God said. It wasn't something he just decided to do on his own. He heard from God and then acted on what he heard. It was a work of faith.

LEARN TO HEAR GOD'S VOICE FOR YOURSELF

Many people become involved in works of the flesh by doing something they see someone else do, instead of following the Lord for themselves. Each person has to learn to hear God's voice for himself. For you, it's not enough that I hear God. You need to hear God for yourself.

So when Abraham heard what God said, he acted on it. He took Isaac up on the mountain and proceeded to do exactly what God told him to do. (Gen. 22:3-10.) Then the Lord spoke to Abraham and said, "No, don't do it. I have made provision. There's a ram in the bush to sacrifice instead." (vv. 11-13.)

ISAAC AND ISHMAEL— LIVING FAITH VERSUS DEAD FAITH

God will always supply a "ram in the thicket"—a divine provision—for you, but you must act on your faith before you will receive it. Your work of faith is to find out what God said, believe it and then begin taking action based on your belief. First find out what God has promised you, and then do something about it. Look at the difference between Ishmael and Isaac's actions. Ishmael represents a work of the flesh, and Isaac represents a work of faith. Let me show you why.

God had promised Abraham a son, but before the promise was fulfilled, Sarah said to Abraham, "Maybe God intends for you to have a child outside of my body. Look how old I am. I'll give you my servant girl, and you can conceive a child with her." (Gen. 16:2.) Abraham agreed, and they had a baby all right—but it was not by a work of faith. It was by a work of the flesh. That baby was Ishmael, and the Bible tells us that Ishmael was not a son of promise. (Gal. 4:28.) Ishmael was not a manifestation of God's grace. Instead, Ishmael was a product of the work of the flesh.

Eventually, however, Abraham and Sarah had faith in what God had promised and believed Him for the birth of their promised son, Isaac. Sarah bore Isaac from her own body just as God had said.

Let's look in the book of Romans for the key to receiving God-kind of results from works of faith.

> **(As it is written, I have made thee [Abraham] a father of many nations,) before him whom he believed, even God, who quickeneth the dead, and calleth those things which be not as though they were. Who against hope believed in hope, that he might become the father of many nations, according to that which was spoken, So shall thy seed be. And being not weak in faith, he considered not his own body now dead, when he was about an hundred years old, neither yet the deadness of Sarah's womb.**

> **Romans 4:17-19**

Initially, Abraham looked at the state of Sarah's body and his own body and thought that all natural hope for a child was gone. Then, the Bible says, he entered into supernatural hope. Where did this supernatural hope come from? Romans 4:18 says that he heard the word that was spoken. Abraham received supernatural hope from the word of God that was spoken to him, and that word was enough for him to hold fast to the promise of God.

The Bible says Abraham didn't consider his own body as dead when he was about one hundred years old. And he didn't consider the barrenness of Sarah's womb either. In the natural, there was no evidence that there was ever going to be a baby from Abraham's and Sarah's union. But Abraham chose not to consider his natural circumstances. And you can choose to do the same thing in your life.

We could read Romans 4:19 this way: "And being not weak in faith, you consider not your *marriage* now dead. You consider not your *finances* now dead. You consider not your *body* now dead. You consider not your *career* now dead." You consider "not dead" whatever it is the devil has lied to you about, telling you it was dead!

LIVE FAITH IS ELECTRIFIED BY PRAISING GOD

Rather than considering his circumstances, Abraham chose instead to praise God.

> He [Abraham] staggered not at the promise of God through unbelief; but was strong in faith, giving glory to God; and being fully persuaded that, what he had promised, he was able also to perform.
>
> **Romans 4:20,21**

Abraham praised and thanked God that He had made him the "father of many nations," even though Abraham didn't have any evidence of it. Abraham operated in faith, and his faith allowed him to access the grace of God. It was

God's grace—His anointing and power—that brought about Isaac's supernatural birth.

God's grace is also available for you! If Abraham could receive a miracle that was so impossible for him, you, too, can receive the miracle that seems impossible in your life. God's grace is just as available to you as it was to Abraham! Your faith gives you the same access into God's grace that Abraham's faith did. Abraham believed the word that was spoken, and he received a miracle from God as a result. Likewise, as you believe in God's Word, you also can receive your promise from God.

What distinguishes the works of the flesh from the works of faith or of grace? Hearing from God is the key difference. For example, if you see someone in a service run to the front and throw an offering of money on the altar, it is only a work of faith if the Holy Spirit prompted that person to do that. If the Holy Spirit did, in fact, prompt that person to do that, then it will put him into position to receive a manifestation of grace in the area of his need.

On the other hand, if you went up to throw money on the altar—above and beyond your tithes—only because you felt obligated to do it, and not because you were prompted by the Holy Spirit, then it could be a work of the flesh, which will not cause a manifestation of God's grace in your life. You cannot force God to do something. God will never owe you; He will never be a debtor to you. You cannot say, "Well, I'm going to do this, and that's going to force God to give me that." It doesn't work that way.

Something becomes a work of faith when it is done in obedience to the direction of the Lord, as a prompting or leading of the Holy Spirit. When the Spirit of God is moving in a certain direction and the body of Christ is following the leading of the Holy Spirit, great things can happen. Some of our most wonderful services have flowed like that. It has happened, for example, when someone was led by the Holy Spirit to say or do something by faith. And when it's truly done in faith, the Holy Spirit will move, blessing all of us in the service. Everyone is blessed by God's grace at work through the Holy Spirit. It's marvelous. And people get saved, healed, delivered and set free!

The book of James talks about faith and corresponding actions. In other words, if you say you have faith, you must also have works that accompany your faith, or you won't see any results. If you say you're in faith, then there's always going to be something you must do, some action you should take. God has to get you up out of your seat and doing something. He has to get you to go somewhere, talk to someone, sow some financial seed or praise Him, so that you're acting out your faith. Faith always requires an act. If you're truly in faith, then you're going to be doing some corresponding action.

However, when you do something without the direction or prompting of the Holy Spirit, it's not done in faith; it's just a work of the flesh. It's an Ishmael and not a child of promise, and it won't produce a God-kind of result.

Galatians 5:4 says that you can fall from grace by doing a work of the flesh. You can even turn your church attendance into a work of the flesh. You can come to church out of obligation and a sense of duty, but when that happens, it ceases to be an act of faith. You won't get much out of church if you come with that kind of attitude.

A RIGHT MOTIVE CAN PRODUCE A RIGHT MANIFESTATION

You have to ask yourself, *Why do I do the things I do?* Even if you give tithes and offerings merely because the Bible says you should, you won't receive a full blessing in return unless you do it in faith. You must use your faith to appropriate biblical promises as a result of your obedience. Now, there is a certain blessing in going through the motions because you know it's the right thing to do and you are simply being obedient. But, if you just do something because you know you should, you are missing out on so much more that God has for you.

Manifestations of biblical promises from the Word of God come as a result of God's grace. We know that you can't earn anything from God. God only asks you to believe Him. God desires that a heart of faith and expectancy motivates you to do what you do. If you do something because you love God and you believe His promises, you're going to see God move on your behalf.

Let me put it another way: Second Corinthians 6:1 says, **We then, as workers together with him, beseech you also**

that ye receive not the grace of God in vain. You can receive the grace of God in vain or nullify it by your works of the flesh.

When I was teaching the Bible at Eastern Michigan University as a college student, I helped to found a college ministry called USC—United Students for Christ—along with Pastor Joe Fry of Great Faith Christian Center in Ann Arbor. One day we were teaching on giving, and a student came up to me and asked, "Does the Bible talk about a hundredfold return?" He said, "I'm going to give away my car, and I figure that the value of my car multiplied by a hundred is a lot of money; I'm going to be rich!"

I said, "Don't you do that. If you do, you're going to end up walking and you won't have a car at all." You see, this young man wasn't doing something in faith because God told him to do it or even out of a heart of love. He was doing it because he was thinking that he would get a hundredfold return and be rich. Do you know what he did? He gave his car away, and he ended up walking for two years until he could manage to get another car.

Now, someone else acting in faith and not out of greed might give a car away and receive a brand-new car in return. This happened once at my Atlanta church. One of my members came up to me and said the Lord had told him to give away his Ford Explorer to another church member who was believing God for a car. So that's what he did. He gave away his Ford Explorer in faith.

Months later, he came up to me and said, "I have to tell you what happened. Someone gave me a brand-new Mercedes Benz S500." What a blessing! That kind of blessing is exactly what the Bible says will happen when you hear from God, exercise a work of faith and receive access into His grace!

Remember, the difference between works of the flesh and works of faith is in your hearing from God. When you hear from Him and cooperate with His principles in faith, you will get results. That's how faith and grace work together. You can't stop the grace of God when you're following God's principles.

CHAPTER 8

GRACE IN
FINANCES

The grace of God is available for us in every area of our lives, including our finances. Because we live in a world that is run by money, we must have money to survive. But even though we live *in* the world, we're not *of* the world. (John 17:15,16.) God is our source, and He is able to supply our needs. (Phil. 4:19.) He is able to take good care of us when we obey what His Word says.

> **Therefore I say unto you, take no thought for your life, what ye shall eat, or what ye shall drink; nor yet for your body, what ye shall put on. Is not the life more than meat, and the body than raiment? Behold the fowls of the air: for they sow not, neither do they reap, nor gather into barns; yet your heavenly Father feedeth them. Are ye not much better than they?**
>
> **Matthew 6:25,26**

According to this passage of Scripture, in God's sight we are so much more valuable than a pigeon. Jesus didn't die for a pigeon. In fact, He didn't die for any animal. No animal has ever been redeemed. Jesus died for people.

Jesus repeats the phrase, "take no thought," five times in Matthew 6. So, let's take a look at what that phrase means. Today, instead of "take no thought," we would say, "Don't worry about it." So, you could read this passage, "Don't worry about what to eat, drink or put on your body." In other words, we don't have to worry about money anymore.

> **Therefore take no thought, saying, What shall we eat? or, What shall we drink? or, Wherewithal shall we be clothed? (For after all these things do the Gentiles seek:) for your heavenly Father knoweth that ye have need of all these things. But seek ye first the kingdom of God, and his righteousness; and all these things shall be added unto you.**
>
> **Matthew 6:31-33**

Who is Jesus talking about when he refers to "Gentiles" in verse 32? Jesus is talking about a person without God in his life. People who don't have God worry about what they are going to eat and what they are going to wear. They question, "What are we going to do? Where are we going to get the money we need? Where are we going to get food? Where are we going to get clothing to wear?"

But we as Christians do know God, and He told us to seek His kingdom—His way of doing things. He also told us to seek His righteousness. That means we are to copy the example of obedience Jesus gave to us. When we do, we can receive all of the things we need in life.

GRACE IN FINANCES MUST BE RECEIVED, NOT EARNED

Jesus said in Matthew 6 that God takes care of the birds of the air. They don't do anything to earn it. Therefore, how much more will God take care of His people? We don't have to earn His care. The birds don't, and God makes sure they're taken care of. God also clothes the flowers, making them beautiful. And He takes care of the grass that is not even going to be here tomorrow.

God will take care of you! You are His child. You are not without God. He said He already knows you need money. You don't need to struggle to get the money you need. No, you can trust God, knowing that He will supply all of your needs!

God is talking about the normal, natural provisions of life in Matthew 6. This is an area of grace that God has provided for you. As a child of God, your normal, daily provisions of life have already been met, and you don't have to do anything to qualify to receive them! All you have to do is believe God, then let grace take care of the rest.

Knowing that God has already made provision for your needs takes the pressure off you to strive for it. Instead of thinking, *I have to strive with God for more money,* you can rest in the assurance that God has already taken care of it. You can say, "Father, the area of finances is one area of my life for which you've already made provision. You've already said You would provide for me. I'm not without You, so I'm not going to worry about money anymore. The only thing I'm going to say is, 'Thank You for supplying all my needs.'"

Your Father will take care of you. Your Father will provide for you. But sometimes people irresponsibly squander the money that God has provided for them. Then they fret or get mad at God because they're in debt. It's not God's fault they're in debt. They didn't listen to God. God may have been saying, *Don't go there. Don't buy that.* But they were probably thinking they deserved to have whatever it was they bought even though they couldn't afford it. Spending money has nothing to do with whether you deserve something. It has to do with what the Word of God says, what the Holy Spirit is leading you to do at the time and whether you can afford it.

The truth is that the things of God are simple. People are the ones who make them complex. Jesus said that a wise man will take His sayings and do them. But an unwise man won't do what Jesus said. And the unwise man will be wiped out when the storms of life come to him, because he has not built his life on Jesus' commandments. (Matt. 7:24-27.)

All we have to do is obey Jesus' commandments. One thing that Jesus commanded us not to do was worry. We should not worry about our daily needs in life, such as food and clothing. Jesus is the Good Shepherd, and He takes care of His sheep. (John 10:11.)

A GOOD FATHER KNOWS WHAT HIS CHILDREN NEED AND PROVIDES IT FOR THEM

I am a father of three children. When my kids were growing up, they didn't need to come to me and ask, "Daddy, will you please buy me some food? Will you please give me some clothes so I don't have to go to school naked?"

No, I already knew my kids needed to eat. I already knew they needed clothes. So, I just went out and got them what they needed. They didn't have to ask me for anything!

I determined to make sure they were well taken care of because that's my role as a father. A good father automatically takes care of his family. When I was a child, with my own daddy, I never had to think about whether or not I was going to be taken care of. My daddy always took good care of us. I never thought about it; I just accepted it.

One of my daughters told me one time, "Daddy, what's yours is mine, and what's mine is mine!" She just assumed that whatever was in my pocket belonged to her. This is true for all my children. They assume that whatever is in my bank account belongs to them, and they don't have any shame whatsoever in asking for it. If they see something they want, they say, "Daddy, I want that."

I often say, "I taught you how to believe God. Believe God for it yourself."

They respond by saying, "Daddy, you know and I know you are going to get that for me!"

My youngest daughter was believing God for a certain kind of car, and she let me know about it.

"I'm not buying that car," I told her. "That car is too expensive."

She put her hands on her hips, looked at me and said, "Now, Daddy, you know and I know that you are going to buy me that car."

Well, guess what kind of car is in the driveway? That car! She didn't have any shame, because she knows that her daddy loves her and her daddy is going to take care of all her basic provisions—and then some!

Well, God is *your* Father, and He knows about your basic provisions and needs. What makes you think that you have to go before Him and cry and beg to get what is yours? You don't. It is God's grace that provides for you, just as it is my grace that takes care of my children!

WHY WORK?

Faith recognizes the character of God and makes a decision to believe God's Word—to believe that God will meet all of your needs. But does this mean that you should never have to work at a job to earn money? God's Word gives a clear answer.

Neither give place to the devil. Let him that stole steal no more: but rather let him labour,

**working with his hands the thing which is good,
that he may have to give to him that needeth.**

Ephesians 4:27,28

We are not to give the devil any openings in our lives. And one way we close the door to the enemy is by working—not for a living, but for a giving.

Notice that Ephesians 4:28 warns against stealing. Is Paul saying that Christians steal? Yes, many Christians steal in subtle ways. They may put their feet up and slack off when their boss leaves the office. These Christians only start working hard when their boss shows up again. They aren't giving their boss a hundred percent when he's out of the office. And then they wonder why they aren't enjoying the blessings of God!

One of the reasons we are to work is so we can give to those who are lacking. (Prov. 28:27.) God honors our giving, and He will repay us. Our source is not our job. God is our source, and our Father God takes care of our provisions as we work to sow seed into other people's lives.

Some people mention 2 Thessalonians 3:10 and say that Paul is telling the Thessalonians that they must work in order to have sustenance in life. Let's look at the whole context of that Scripture.

For even when we were with you, this we commanded you, that if any would not work, neither should he eat.

2 Thessalonians 3:10

Throughout this passage of Scripture, Paul had been talking about disorderly conduct. He was addressing people who were going into the camp, sitting around, getting into everyone else's business, sleeping in everyone else's houses, and eating everyone else's food. These people were idle busybodies who needed correction. When Paul said that if a man doesn't work, he shouldn't eat, he was not saying that an individual has to labor in order to have sustenance in his life. God will provide sustenance. A man should work in order to be a blessing to others.

It's disorderly for someone to come and just hang around your house for a lengthy period of time and not contribute anything to your household. I was in Washington, D.C., once with my whole family, and a guy about twenty-five years old approached me and said, "Hey, brother, why don't you give me some money?"

This young man was tall and muscular. I said, "Get a job, and get your own money." That boy was healthier than I was! I wasn't going to give him any money, but I would have given him a job. In fact, I went back to that young panhandler and said, "I'll give you work. I have a church, and I have some things you can do. And I'll pay you." The guy didn't take my offer. He just wanted a handout.

HOW TO ABOUND IN THE GRACE OF GIVING

Let's look at a group of people who didn't operate out of works but, instead, abounded in grace by their giving.

> **Moreover, brethren, we do you to wit of the grace of God bestowed on the churches of Macedonia; how that in a great trial of affliction the abundance of their joy and their deep poverty abounded unto the riches of their liberality. For to their power, I bear record, yea, and beyond their power they were willing of themselves.**
>
> **2 Corinthians 8:1-3**

In this Scripture, Paul is talking about grace, specifically about how the favor of God was revealed in the churches at Macedonia. They suffered deep poverty, but they gave of themselves in every way regardless. They abounded in the grace of giving despite their situation.

What motivates people to give beyond their means like the churches of Macedonia? To put it simply: love does. The Macedonians gave the way they did because they loved people. They weren't worried about their needs being met. They already knew that God was going to supply their needs, so they took what they had and gave it to those who needed help. Their faith working by love accessed the grace of God. (Gal. 5:6.)

> **Therefore I thought it necessary to exhort the brethren, that they would go before unto you, and make up beforehand your bounty, whereof ye had notice before, that the same might be ready, as a matter of bounty, and not as of covetousness. But this I say, He which soweth sparingly shall reap**

also sparingly; and he which soweth bountifully shall reap also bountifully. Every man according as he purposeth in his heart, so let him give; not grudgingly, or of necessity: for God loveth a cheerful giver. And God is able to make all grace abound toward you; that ye, always having all sufficiency in all things, may abound to every good work.

2 Corinthians 9:5-8

In verse 6, Paul explains the principle of giving and receiving. He says that if you give a little, you will receive a little. But if you give much, you will receive much.

In verse 7, Paul talks about the motive for giving. Your motivation should be one of love mixed with faith. You shouldn't give your tithes with the thought, *I plan to have this multiplied back to me within a week.* God's Word does say you will be blessed when you give. But I'm referring to the real motive behind what you do. The Corinthians gave, knowing God would supply their needs. They gave from the depth of love in their hearts and their desire to help the church at Macedonia. That's the way true givers should be motivated.

You should be giving offerings so that the Word you hear can also be heard by someone else, because you want someone else to be blessed with the Word of God. You should not be giving because you want to get money back, but your heart motive should be to bless others.

Second Corinthians 9:8 says that God is able to make all grace abound toward you. As we have already seen, grace is favor, the power of the Holy Spirit, blessing, help, mercy, lovingkindness, anointing, generosity, revelation of the Word, healing, preservation and soundness. God is therefore able to make all grace—all these things—abound toward you so that you will always have the sufficiency you need in all things. What else does the term "all things" include? It not only includes financial blessings, but also blessings in your marriage, your family, your wisdom and understanding or anything else you might need.

God's grace can abound toward you so that you'll have more money with which to bless more people. When you begin to do things for others as directed by the Holy Spirit and motivated out of a heart of love and faith, you then become open to receive in your own life from any area of grace that you are in need of. When you are acting out of love, then you are acting like God Himself. When you begin acting like God Himself, then you can believe for anything God has to be given to you.

When you act in faith and love in order to help someone else, you release the grace of God to abound toward you in every area of your life. However, if you can only believe for a financial return, then that's all you'll get! You can choose to believe for all the rest of God's blessings as well. When you sow your seed to God, you cannot say, "God, you owe me this certain amount because I put my money in here." God doesn't owe you anything! If you can believe God will pour out His grace in every area of your life when you sow your seed, then you can receive from God immeasurably and be blessed abundantly.

> But I have all, and abound: I am full, having
> received of Epaphroditus the things which were
> sent from you, an odour of a sweet smell, a sacri-
> fice acceptable, wellpleasing to God. But my God
> shall supply all your need according to his riches
> in glory by Christ Jesus.
>
> Philippians 4:18,19

In Philippians 4:18-19, Paul is talking to the church at Philippi, telling them the same thing he told the Corinthians. He is saying, "When you give something to help someone else, God will open up areas of grace in your own life." It has nothing to do with works, but everything to do with faith!

One of the biggest needs the body of Christ faces right now is grace in the area of finances. And the answer to this need is found in the Word of God. Believers must know that everything they have comes by the grace of God.

Satan will attempt to deprive you of what is rightfully yours. He'll get in the way and try to stop what's coming to you. But you can receive all God has provided for you by using your faith to claim what's yours!

Instead of just working for a paycheck, you can claim an amount that you need or want by faith. Then tell the devil to take his hands off your money, and tell your angel to go get it, because it has already been provided. The grace for it is already there. I learned this from Kenneth E. Hagin years ago in a message entitled, "How God Taught Me About Prosperity." The Lord appeared to him and told him to lay claim to what was already his. The Lord told him not to pray about money anymore the way he had been praying for it. This is very different from laboring for your money! There is grace in finances, and once you tap into it, you can live abundantly!

CHAPTER 9

MAINTAINING
THE GRACE

N ow that we've seen all that grace can be, let's look at how to maintain it and keep a constant flow of it in our lives. First of all, you must be convinced that the grace of God is truly yours, that it already belongs to you. Unless you are totally convinced that God's grace with all its provision is yours, you are not going to receive a full measure of it. Secondly, you must realize that there are things you can do to keep the flow of grace operating in your life. The actions that you take will determine the promises of God that you will receive. Remember, faith is an act. So you need to do something to receive the promise. With that in mind, let's look at exactly what you need to do to maintain God's grace.

CONTINUE TO HEAR

The first thing you must do is to continue to hear the word of grace. Faith comes by hearing and hearing by the Word of God. (Rom. 10:17.) You need to be in church each week, rather than sitting in front of the television. If it's at all possible, you should be *in* the house of God, hearing God's Word and building your faith.

Now, if you can't get to church, then watch a service on television. But you need to get the Word of grace inside of you regularly. Expose yourself to the Word. It's not enough to do it just once. Continually put yourself in a position to hear the Word of God, particularly the Word of God that addresses what you need for your situation. For example, if you have a physical limitation, you need to feed yourself God's Word on the subject of healing. Keep listening to the Word on healing; keep speaking the Word on healing. Faith comes by hearing the Word of God.

CONTINUE TO BELIEVE

Secondly, you need to believe the Word of God as proof of what you don't see. (Heb. 11:1.) The Word of God *is* your proof.

If your checkbook is empty, God's Word still says, "You are provided for." (Phil. 4:19.) If your situation looks like divorce, God's Word still says that love never fails. (1 Cor. 13:8.) If the world says that you can't, God's Word still says, "You can do all things through Christ." (Phil. 4:13.)

There are more than 7,000 promises in the Word of God available to you. Get into the Word to find the Scripture that covers your situation. Find the Word that you need; then believe that the Word of God is the proof of what you don't see. Instead of looking at the situation, continue to look at the Word.

CONTINUE TO SPEAK

Thirdly, you need to boldly speak words of hope and encouragement that are based on the Word of God. Make sure you don't change those words. Speak what the Word says, not what the circumstances say. Hebrews 3:1 says, **Consider the Apostle and High Priest of our profession, Christ Jesus.** Understand that Jesus, the High Priest of your words, takes what you say before the throne of grace, causing mercy and grace to come to your aid just when you need it.

When you start speaking out what God says about something, all hell may break loose to get you off track. For example, if you start confessing, "I walk in love, and I'm not going to be in strife with my brethren," then you can bet Satan will try to bring someone along to offend you and tempt you to get out of faith.

The area in which you need to receive grace is the area your confession should focus on. For example, if you're standing for your healing, you should be saying, "I'm the healed and not the sick! From the crown of my head to the soles of my feet, every organ, every tissue in my body functions perfectly according to the way God created it to function. Thank You, Father, that my brain is healed, my stomach is healed, my liver is healed, my colon is healed, my pancreas is healed, my heart is healed, my blood pressure is normal and stays normal, my skin is pure and my blood is pure."

When you start speaking forth what God's Word says about your body, the enemy may try to shoot pain at you, but you don't have to listen to the enemy. He might even try to bring sickness to your body, but that doesn't mean you need to believe it.

That happened to me once. I was in the shower when I noticed a large lump beneath my arm. Every day I got up, and that lump was still there. It became more painful, and it seemed to get bigger. It started off the size of a penny, and it kept growing until it became a sizable knot under my arm.

I made a determination not to change my confession. I did not start saying, "This could be cancer. I know someone else who had that." I didn't let fear grab me. I didn't change my words of faith. Healing is not something I have to earn. It has already been provided, and as long as I don't waver in my faith, I'm going to access God's grace. Grace is much more powerful than a lump!

So I just hung in there with my faith and my confession. Every morning when I got up, I said, "In the name of Jesus, I curse every growth, lump, cyst or tumor trying to come against my body. You have no power in my body in Jesus' name."

I'm not telling you to avoid your doctor when you experience symptoms in your body. In fact, you probably should go. I'm just telling you what I did. What I do is not necessarily what you're supposed to do. But whether you go to a doctor or not, you should not change what you say. Going to a doctor does not mean you have lost your faith.

In my case, however, I didn't say anything to anyone about my situation. I didn't even say anything to my wife. I just kept on speaking God's Word. And when I got up one morning, I noticed the lump was gone! When did it leave? I don't know. I do know that it hasn't come back. God's Word is much more powerful than a growth, cyst, lump or tumor. Speak what God's Word says, and don't change your confession.

Seeing then that we have a great high priest, that is passed into the heavens, Jesus the Son of God, let us hold fast our profession. For we have not an high priest which cannot be touched with the feeling of our infirmities; but was in all points tempted like as we are, yet without sin.

Hebrews 4:14,15

Jesus has been where you've been. He knows what it feels like to be you. He knows what it feels like to be attacked by the devil. You don't have to do a thing wrong to be attacked by the devil. You can be doing everything right, and he will still attack you. Jesus didn't tell you that you would not be attacked. He said to be of good cheer because He has overcome—and, therefore, you can overcome—any attack of the enemy! (John 16:33.)

CONTINUE TO GO BOLDLY TO THE THRONE OF GRACE

The fourth thing that you can do to maintain the grace of God in your life is to come boldly to the throne of grace.

> For we have not an high priest which cannot
> be touched with the feeling of our infirmities; but
> was in all points tempted like as we are, yet
> without sin. Let us therefore come boldly unto the
> throne of grace, that we may obtain mercy, and
> find grace to help in time of need.
>
> **Hebrews 4:15,16**

March boldly to the throne in Jesus' name so that you can receive mercy and grace. If you have sinned, God's mercy is available. You will find mercy and grace to help in the time of your need. It will be there right on time!

Our great High Priest understands what we are going through. And at that throne of grace, we can find all the favor, all the anointing, all the power and all the help we could ever need! We can come to the throne of grace, thanking God that we have received whatever it is we may need. And then we can rest assured that God's grace will show up!

The answer to your problem is already there. God is Jehovah-Jireh, the God of provision. He knew that you were going to need help before the situation even developed. And He made provision for you to triumph over that situation before it ever occurred in the first place.

So what is left for us to do to maintain the flow of grace in our lives? Once you have realized that your answer has already been provided, all that's left to do is say "thank you."

CONTINUE TO OFFER THE SACRIFICE
OF PRAISE TO THE LORD

The fifth and final thing required to maintaining grace in your life is to offer the sacrifice of praise and to enter into God's rest.

By him therefore let us offer the sacrifice of praise to God continually, that is, the fruit of our lips giving thanks to his name.

Hebrews 13:15

What does it mean to offer a "sacrifice of praise"? Sometimes you may not feel like praising God, but you do it anyway. When your circumstances look bad, it's not easy to praise God. That's why it's called a "sacrifice of praise."

For example, I didn't feel like praising God when I found that lump beneath my arm. But that was the time I had to say, "I have enough faith and trust in God's Word that I'm not going to give in to this thing. I'm going to praise God, because He is good and because He has already provided my healing."

It is easy to praise God when we're surrounded by believers on Sunday morning. But when we're alone and feeling isolated, that's the time we need to praise God the most—to offer the sacrifice of praise.

I remember when we were believing God for our first church building. The day finally came for us to close on the building, and we did not have the money. We were supposed to close at three o'clock in the afternoon.

I was at our storefront property at 10 A.M. on the day of the closing. The lease on that property was set to expire that weekend, so if we didn't close the deal then, we wouldn't have any place to hold church services. I was walking up and down that storefront, making my confessions of faith as I waited. Then I started rejoicing and praising God. I began jumping up and down and running around the room. At one point, I even rolled around on the floor.

At first, I hadn't felt like praising God. I felt like giving up and quitting. But I just kept praising God anyway. I kept offering the sacrifice of praise to the Lord. After a while, the phone rang. It was an attorney who had visited our church once or twice before. He told me that he was calling from a phone booth, because he couldn't wait to call me from another phone. "The Lord told me to stop and call you," he said. "The Lord told me to come over and bring you a check."

I said, "Come on down!" He showed up fifteen minutes later, bringing his corporate checkbook. He happened to be the owner of a law firm.

"The Lord told me to give you this checkbook," he said. "Take a check and fill in whatever amount you need."

Do you know what I did? I wrote the check for the entire amount I needed, and we closed on the church building!

Now that's an example of God's grace in action! You see, when we come before God, we can praise Him no matter how bad it seems. We can praise God because the situation has already been taken care of. We can come before God in faith, knowing the work is already done. All that's left to do is enter into God's grace and receive your answer.

When you begin to praise God, something wonderful happens. You enter into a place of rest. It's called the "rest of faith," and it's available to you at any time.

> **For unto us was the gospel preached, as well as unto them: but the word preached did not profit them, not being mixed with faith in them that heard it. For we which have believed do enter into rest, as he said, As I have sworn in my wrath, if they shall enter into my rest: although the works were finished from the foundation of the world.**
>
> **Hebrews 4:2,3**

Those who are operating in faith are operating in the rest and peace of God. They are thanking God that as much grace as they need is available whenever they need it! Christians should not worry. They shouldn't have any anxiety, and they shouldn't be trying to make something happen in their own strength. They should just be believing God, thanking Him that every need is met in abundance!

TALK ABOUT THE ANSWER, NOT THE PROBLEM

In Acts 16, Paul was being followed by a demon-possessed girl everywhere he went. She kept saying, "These are the men of the Most High God!" After many days, Paul finally told that demon spirit to come out of her.

125

That upset the men who profited from her soothsaying. So they took Paul and Silas into downtown Macedonia to be beaten, stripped and thrown into prison. The circumstances were bad for Paul and Silas. But what did they do?

And at midnight Paul and Silas prayed, and sang praises unto God: and the prisoners heard them.

Acts 16:25

Paul and Silas prayed the *answer* instead of the *problem*. They must have prayed, "God, they may have beaten us; they may have done us wrong. But it doesn't matter! We know that You can make a way for us. We know You'll open a door for us."

When you pray the answer instead of the problem, you can start singing a song of victory because He has already answered your needs.

That's exactly what Paul and Silas did. In their darkest hour, they began to sing praises unto God, and everyone heard them.

And suddenly there was a great earthquake, so that the foundations of the prison were shaken: and immediately all the doors were opened, and every one's bands were loosed.

Acts 16:26

Suddenly! That's very often the way God works. When something happens suddenly, it happens quickly and instantly. One moment things are one way, but in the next second everything has changed. One minute you're broke, but the next minute you have all the money you need. One minute your husband is acting like a fool, but the next minute he loves the Lord. One minute it looks like your ministry isn't going to work, but the next minute the anointing of God shows up.

It doesn't matter what it looks like; it doesn't matter what's going on right now. Things can change suddenly! God can begin to shake things up in your marriage, your finances, your relationships or in whatever area you have problems.

After the earthquake in Paul's and Silas' jail cell, the prison doors were opened wide. Paul and Silas had a chance to run for their lives, but instead they chose to stay in prison long enough to preach the Gospel to everyone. And as a result, people were saved, sanctified and filled with the Holy Spirit.

When Paul and Silas operated in their faith, it released the grace of God, and the power of the Holy Spirit shook that place. That is exactly how you access the grace of God—by faith! You don't have to work for the grace of God. Jesus already paid the price for you; He did all the work already. All you have to do is believe and receive!

Jesus said that the kingdom of God is like a man who plants seed in the ground. He goes to bed and he gets up. He knows something is coming, but he doesn't know how. But one day that blade comes up through the ground, and then, eventually, it is time to harvest.

You need to thank your heavenly Father that whatever you have believed Him for is already done. You can go to bed and get up and praise God.

Faith is not hard; it's easy. You don't have to work anymore. All you have to do is believe you receive an abundance of grace, and you will reign like a king in this life!

Even though circumstances may tell you that your needs are not going to be met, God's Word says they are. You know that your Father will do what He said. You know you can count on God, because He has already provided for you. It's a finished work and a "done deal"!

You can tell the devil to take his hands off your stuff! You can tell the angels of God to bring back what the devil has stolen. And then you can thank God that it's done. That's how you maintain the grace God has given you.

God doesn't want you to be burdened and overwhelmed with anxiety over anything! He wants you to act on His Word. Not only does God want you free from worry about the circumstances of life, He wants you to be free from worry about spiritual things too.

In Acts 3, a notable miracle took place. Peter and John were walking into the temple when they noticed a crippled man sitting at the gate called Beautiful. The man was hoping to receive something when Peter walked by. Peter told him, "I don't have any silver, and I don't have any gold. But what I do have, I will give to you. In the name of Jesus, rise up and walk."

That man got up and received the strength to walk. He went into the temple, walking, leaping and praising God. Afterward, the whole city was amazed, because everyone knew the formerly crippled man.

Finally, the Sanhedrin counsel said, "If we don't do something about this, this whole Jesus stuff will take over, and everyone will follow Him." So the Sanhedrin counsel forbade Peter to speak in Jesus' name. (Acts 4:18.)

Despite these threats and warnings, Peter and John didn't start talking about the problem. They didn't complain to God about the situation in which they found themselves. Instead, they started praising God. They acknowledged that God made the heavens and earth, and, therefore, all power was in His hand. They acknowledged that nothing was above Him. They magnified the Lord instead of the problem.

The disciples didn't even consider their own problems. Instead, they began to preach with great boldness. (Acts 4:31.) As a result, an abundance of grace showed up for everyone, and the entire place was shaken by the power of the Holy Spirit. Their faith brought so much grace that the whole place shook!

God will use believers to meet the needs of other believers. And as believers obey Him, He will keep pouring out more and more grace until there's an overflowing abundance of it.

Great faith will give you entrance into great grace. When you're operating in faith and love, it creates an atmosphere in which God can move. With God's grace at work, every need can be met in abundance. And with every need being met, you can be encouraged to maintain a constant flow of grace in your life. God wants to see you prosper, and He will give you the grace to make it happen. God's grace really works!

FIVE STEPS TO MAINTAINING GOD'S GRACE

Once you've received God's great provision in your life, you have to keep it there and maintain a constant flow of God's grace. Here's how:

Step One: **Continue to hear the word of grace.**

To ensure God's grace continues to flow, you must keep hearing God's Word. Faith comes by hearing and hearing by the Word of God. (Rom. 10:17.)

Step Two: **Believe God's Word as proof of that which you don't yet see.**

Sometimes you may experience circumstances that seem contrary to God's promises to you. You must believe the Word anyhow. Don't deny that the circumstance is not really there, but do remember that God's Word through faith can change the circumstances. (Heb. 11:1.)

Step Three: **Speak God's Word.**

First you believe, then you speak. Jesus is the High Priest of your confession. (Heb. 3:1.) Therefore, He takes your words spoken in faith and offers them up to the Father as a testimony of your faith.

Step Four: **Offer up praises to God.**

Remember, praising God is faith in advance. When you praise God, you are already thanking Him for supplying all your needs even though you may not see that provision yet. Praise moves the hand of God.

Step Five: **Enter into a place of rest.**

After you've done all that you know to do, rest in the assurance that God is working on your behalf. The Bible says that those of us who believe enter into a rest of faith. (Heb.4:3.) Let God take care of your needs. He's more than able.

The important thing to remember about grace is that it's a gift. It's free. All you have to do is receive it by faith. You can't exhaust God's grace. He has enough grace to heal you. He has enough grace to prosper you. He has enough grace to set you free. There's no limit to the amount of grace you can receive from God!

So just relax and enjoy God's grace. You're somebody special to God. You don't have to work for anything God has. He has already given it to you because He loves you. So, just begin to thank Him for it. Thank God for that which is already yours. You can go to bed praising God. You can get up the next day praising Him. Start praising God throughout your day, and you'll find words of faith coming out of your mouth. Words of doubt will disappear, and you'll find the power of God, the health and healing of God, the joy of God and the very grace of God manifesting itself in your life.

ENDNOTES

Chapter 1

[1] Vaughan.

[2] Ibid.

[3] Ibid.

[4] Ibid.

Chapter 2

[1] Vaughan.

Chapter 3

[1] *Webster's New World College Dictionary,* 3d Ed., s.v. "reward."

[2] Ibid.

[3] Strong, "Greek," entry #4397.

[4] Ibid.

[5] *Webster's New World College Dictionary,* 3d Ed., s.v. "buffet."

[6] Vaughan.

Chapter 4

[1] Strong, "Greek," entry #4982.

[2] Ibid.

[3] Ibid.

[4] *Webster's New World College Dictionary,* 3d Ed., s.v. "faith."

[5] Strong, "Greek," entry #4992.

[6] *Webster's New World College Dictionary,* 3d Ed., s.v. "consolation."

Chapter 5

[1] Strong, "Greek," entry #2842.

REFERENCES

Strong, James. *Strong's Exhaustive Concordance of the Bible.* "Greek Dictionary of the New Testament." Nashville: Abingdon, 1890.

Vaughan, Curtis. *The Emphasized New Testament* as cited in *The Word, The Bible From 26 Translations.* 1988.

Webster's New World College Dictionary, 3d Edition. New York: Macmillan, 1996.

ABOUT THE AUTHOR

Bishop Keith A. Butler is the founder and senior pastor of Word of Faith International Christian Center.

Word of Faith International Christian Center was founded on January 14, 1979, and is a congregation of 16,000 plus members and 200 employees. The main church is located on a beautiful 110-acre campus in Southfield, Michigan, where multiple services are held in the 5,000 seat auditorium. He also pastors Faith Christian Centers in Smyrna, Georgia, which began in August 1993 and in Phoenix, Arizona, which began in September 1997.

Bishop Butler is a pastor and a Bible teacher with ministerial emphasis on teaching line-by-line and applying God's Word to people's daily lives. He ministers in seminars, conventions and churches throughout the country and in third-world nations.

Bishop Butler is an author and conference speaker who travels all over the world. He and his lovely wife, Deborah, have three children who are all active in the work of the ministry: Pastor and Mrs. Keith A. Butler II, Minister MiChelle Butler and Ms. Kristina Butler.

You may contact Keith Butler
by writing:

Word of Faith Publications
P.O. Box 3247
Southfield, Michigan 48037-3247

www.wordoffaithicc.org

*Please include
your prayer requests
and comments when you write.*

THE HARRISON HOUSE VISION

Proclaiming the truth and the power
Of the Gospel of Jesus Christ
With excellence;

Challenging Christians to
Live victoriously,
Grow spiritually,
Know God intimately.